THE GAME

Stuart Roy Clarke

with

John Williams
University of Leicester, England

In putting together this book, I asked myself of each page,
'Will this make you smile in North America?'

Foreword

BY HUNTER DAVIES

Author of the only authorized biography of the Beatles

The moon's a balloon, or is it a ball? Strange how so many shapes in nature, on Earth and in the heavens, are round, sort of circular, a bit like a ball. Right back to the birth of time.

A pity Stuart Roy Clarke was not around earlier to capture those early versions of the game, but he has rather made up for it in these last thirty years, observing football playing, football loving, football influences, with an eye, imagination, and sensitivity which no other football photographer in my long-legged experience has ever bettered.

I first came across him about thirty years ago, in the English Lake District. He had this marvelous place full of photographs and curious papier-mâché figures - including a flying goalkeeper - on the corner of a street in the beautiful town of Ambleside.

It turned out to be more of a museum, a series of displays on the national game. Entry free, but of course you could buy prints and postcards. Over the years I bought loads of his postcards, eagerly awaiting his next endeavors. I loved every one. I don't think I have seen a boring, or bad, or dull Stuart Roy Clarke football image. They make me smile, because many are so witty; or they make me feel sad, looking at those poor sods trudging home in the rain having been stuffed once again. Or they make me think, because so often Stuart finds an oblique angle for a well-known football ritual, such as kickoff, or even the teams lining up.

One thing about football, something which makes it so loved across the world, is that when you go to a game you feel you are communing with everyone or anyone who has ever played or ever gone to a game, anywhere, at any time, since the laws, as we still know them, were first defined in 1863. Where the game is taking place, the language, the climate, the terrain, are all irrelevant. You understand what is going on, how everyone feels.

At any game, amateur kick-about or professional match, I like to think that I am experiencing what people in the past have experienced – and will experience again in the future. We are all members of the football family. And Stuart Roy Clarke is our archivist, recording our family fun and our deepest soulful, heartfelt football feelings. Long may he continue to do so.

Chapters

Introduction

Throughout this book, because we are Brits, we are going to refer to the game as football, even though many of our readers call it soccer.

Stuart Roy Clarke (**SRC**) and University of Leicester Associate Professor in Sociology John Williams (**JW**) have known each other for thirty years.

While Stuart has been taking and exhibiting photographs of football stadiums and the people in and around the game during that time, John has been writing about the game and the fans who watch it for academic journals and books.

This is their first collaboration. The conversations which follow took place in Leicester, bringing about the book *THE GAME*. Enthused about what they had produced and thinking the book had not gone far enough, once it had sold out they added a further conversation and photographs for 2020.

These conversations are designed to explore the history of football in Britain, the people who made it, and the role of photography in extending our understanding and enjoyment of a sporting activity and obsession that now extends across the world. We hope you enjoy reading our conversations as much as we did kicking around ideas about the roots and meaning of the global sport.

CHAPTER 1

And Fate Handed Us The Ball

SRC: Let's begin at the beginning. I like to think of the coming of football as like a great meteorite hitting the earth. We couldn't really avoid it. *Boom!* Like it happened in one day and the game was almost waiting to be played on this planet since it started spinning. There is something metaphysical about why we all play the game, surely. Look at the ball's organic, natural shape. Circular forms like this have been worshiped, cared for, and kicked around since before records began, and well before the coming of photographic evidence. *Fate handed us the ball.*

Football was always going to happen: it was just a question of when and where... and how it would be played. England and that northern part of it where I have lived for so long, Cumbria, where Hunter Davies first came across me, claims it as *theirs*. Being even more specific, one could locate the epicenter of the original football arousal in that stoic old place of Workington, out there on the Cumberland coast. Perhaps Workington is to football what Windsor is to the monarchy. The difference being nobody goes to the *working-town* to discover this.

JW: Is it significant that we have some impressive early examples of local 'folk' football matches surviving today in the UK? Some go back a few hundred years and others – like your Workington example – much longer. You seem to have made a beeline for them with your camera, to include them alongside the more marketable, familiar, and modern versions of the game.

SRC: I can't escape it: 'primitive' football is all around me it seems – in Cumbria, the Lake District, where they have 'Uppies and Downies,' and then, lo and behold, when I moved to Derbyshire in the English Midlands there was the more celebrated Royal Ashbourne game 'Uppards and Downards' on my doorstep. I would say to anyone, 'COME ALONG! You will know as much about this as me;

'Ball On The Village Green' - Elsdon, Northumbria, England, 2000
(SRC)

it's all played out in front of us.'

After all, these earthy sporting battles, which some people may even think of as barbaric, are SO simple: you either play for the team going *UP*, or their counterparts going *DOWN*. There are no clear sides – anyone can play for anyone – at Workington it's traditionally Colliers kicking uphill versus Sailors kicking down.

In the early 1800s, at places around Sheffield, an English city, which has claims to be the cradle of the modern game, sides were based on distinctions such as married men versus not-married men. Today it may be married men versus divorced men. Or women. Anyhow, what I am trying to put across is that it's not a far cry from those jumpers-for-goalposts and school playground games where two captains pick their team based on who they like and don't like, preference for bigger kids, whatever. I am telling you this because no one ever goes there (Workington) to find out.

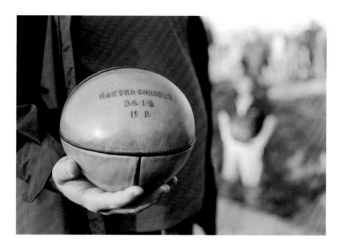

'Hand Crafted With Honor' - Uppies and Downies, Workington, England, 2015
(SRC)

JW: I like the fact that some of the young guys who play in these Uppies v Downies football contests in a handful of places up and down the country wear football shirts drawn from today's professional clubs, giving some connection to the modern game. They play not for reward, but rather for bragging rights. Or even for something we, the general population, can't quite grasp because it is now such a rare experience – playing for our people. However, I do get the feeling that in a world of branding and tourist this-and-that, there is something quite refreshing surely in this media-free zone.

SRC: Imagine it: it's Easter-time. We are back at Workington. An hour to kickoff. There is NO crowd and certainly nobody buying or selling tickets; then a trickle of people turns into a flood. They are all locals. You would not be surprised to see Boudicca arrive on a chariot bearing THE ball. It's a soft leather cherished thing stitched (and what an honor to do so) by a local craftsman. It will be kicked, thumped, crushed under the weight of hefty blokes. It must NOT burst or have its innards fall out. Here the game takes as long as it takes – people go home, return to base, make an egg and bacon sandwich, have a kip, awake with love bites or to domestic disputes, walk the dog… then get back out there looking for the game they left hours ago. It could be anywhere around town.

This game that always starts in the light is invariably pitched into complete darkness for much of it – and it's hard to see the ball. Which could lead to abuse. Where, for hundreds of years there were categorically NO rules in the Workington game, they recently introduced just one: you can't put the ball in a car and drive off. Because someone did.

But make no mistake; there's honor among 'no rules.' The players have their own code of conduct – they have to, as there are no referees, no commentators and the police stand well clear. There is practically no press coverage nor post-match analysis, save for bar talk.

JW: Theories abound about how we eventually moved on from the local versions of this wild Workington game, played on the land, across rivers and in the streets with no written rules. How did we get from here to modern football, with a specified number of players per side, an agreed pitch size and markings, and a more civilized and 'fair' approach to playing sport?

'One Or The Other' - Uppies and Downies, Workington, 2015
(SRC)

SRC: How convenient it would be if we could just say that after the shambolic sprawling rabble-rousing street matches, working-class people militantly, yet lovingly, set up factory clubs and organized their own teams. Indeed, this is what I thought was the universal truth when I was growing up. This was because our local youth football leagues around Watford were dominated by canny Scottish folk who had come south mainly from Lanarkshire, to find work in modern factories such as Atlas Copco, Lucas Aerospace, Kodak, etc. And in my mind these men saw the *fitba'* as an area in their lives where they could take control, boss it, do something meaningful outside of work and – being good organizers – they could create a legacy for their children and for the children of others like them.

'Can't Be Put In A Car' - Uppies and Downies, Workington, 2015
(SRC)

JW: Respect is due to the Scots who so informed your youth, who did indeed produce so many organizers and managers of the game, but football's narrative is even more fascinating and more complicated than any one story.

Some historians argue that the English public schools and ex-schoolboys produced written rules for the handling and kicking games and then tried to spread them among working-class people around Britain.

Others argue that in places in England such as East Lancashire, Sheffield, and the Midlands, working people had already produced their own organized football culture and had devised local rules. They would soon recruit and pay working class Scottish 'professors,' maestros of the feet and early natural team players, to advance the game and their local clubs.

SRC: Perhaps the two teams of historians should have a match to decide who is right!

JW: From 1863, the men who formed the world's first Football Association in London slowly began to exert national control by ironing out regional differences and producing a simple set of written laws that all supporters of the kicking game could understand. 'Hacking' would have to go – to the rugby field. We eventually had a national game to take to the world.

The game soon produced its early star performers. The professional version wasn't far away. Football, in evolutionary terms, just *had* to evolve and spread – it couldn't always be based on local bragging rights and on playing in the style of 'what used to be.'

SRC: The legendary Liverpool manager Bill Shankly used to say about football: 'All you need is the sky, a ball, and the grass.' Or no grass. Some of my earliest football memories are about images of working-class footballers – Ashington's Bobby and Jackie Charlton – back in the fifties, playing with local kids in northern backstreets and alleyways. They did their stuff on knee-bruising concrete or cobbles. Shankly understood what football meant to his local pit village, but he could also see how the simple game could touch everyone's lives. He was a native scientist AND a captain and a manager. He applied nuclear fission to football. *Bill split the football atom!*

By the 1960s monochrome had turned into color in every home. At the moment that the human race was reaching for the stars with a space program (which wasn't just a match between the Old Firm of the USA and Russia), Scotland had produced a truly great Celtic team. Even Northern Ireland showcased George Best, a man from a different planet. British football now seemed fueled by a genuinely optimistic mood that everything might be possible and could be reached for.

'Football Kit Of Sorts' - Uppies and Downies, Workington, 2015
(SRC)

JW: I suspect this is not the last we'll hear about George. He was his own shooting star and, in some ways, he helped create the landscape for today's moneyed version of global football. The young Best certainly drove color into the English game and he drove his various managers to distraction while doing it. Your enthusiasm for George strikes me as part of the paradox of your work: that on the one hand you want to record 'the Best effect,' football reaching for the stars. But on the other, many of your

Manchester United footballer George Best shows manager Sir Matt Busby
his European Footballer of the Year Award at Old Trafford, 1969
(Mirrorpix)

photographs are so down to earth they also excavate its deep roots, the part that has little celebrity or glamor. You enjoy those tribal players of Workington, none of whom are star material, playing their dirty street game. But when the all-singing-all-dancing Premier League comes along, you want to embrace that too.

Your photographs show us that ALL are welcome in the football pleasure-dome. It is part of the enduring beauty and intrigue of fandom and football that they work so well on so many different levels.

SRC: The ball being that one thing that they all have in common. For me, the whole darned world is a football pitch – and football values are never very far away.

Look at that aerial view of Hackney Marshes in London and its 88 pitches. If not God Himself, then a god of football is surely looking down on this sporting landscape. The marshes are the grand epitome of the sort of place where, all over the country, young guys still do their regular Sunday-morning battle. A player might boot the ball up-field not realizing it's the ball from the pitch next door: two balls on the field. Scowling and laughing ensue. All part of the dualism of the game.

JW: Hackney Marshes does look like a vast geometric homage to pleasure and play. It is an extreme example. It is the altar of the grassroots game (albeit built on bomb-damaged rubble). Anyone can play.

Hackney Marshes in East London, 1987, built on marsh filled with bombed building rubble after World War II
(Mirrorpix)

8

The 1957-58 Burnt Ash football team in Bromley - David Jones,
before he became Bowie, is seated on the far left.
(Courtesy of Burnt Ash Primary School, Kent, England)

SRC: There is a lovely school team photo from the late fifties involving, unlikely as this might seem, David Bowie. It reminds us that most British boys probably played some sort of football back then. It's the kind of memento that lots of men in Britain of a certain age will have in a box in the attic, on discreet show somewhere, or else locked away safely. I know yours, John, is above your downstairs toilet cistern! You see it every time you flush. Photographs like these are elegiac, reminding you of the passing of the years. Chalking the year on the ball locates the image time-wise, but it also gives the picture a kind of timeless quality.

JW: Sadly, local schools playing football – my toilet photo – seems to have got lost in this country. Most kids in state schools today will probably never get to experience that amazing feeling of representing your school at football.

In the 1960s in Liverpool, where the locals could lay claim to the game itself, as junior school kids if we had a match to play in the evening we could wear our tangerine football shirts to school, under our jumpers. Very proud we were. We had some tough rivalries: Protestant schools (that orange connection) taking on our Catholic nemeses. I guess we did come together, become a sort of Liverpool united, when we played representative matches against the Manchester schools.

SRC: For me, this is an essential part of the tribal nature of the game. You always need identifiable rivals – invaders –

to make it work best. It was those local rivalries that made the early forms of folk football so brutal and which gives the game an edge today, and probably will do tomorrow.

JW: Yet the beauty of organized football is that you can never entirely play your own game; you always have to take account of the opposition. The national team didn't always seem to get that message. When England lost 1-0 to the USA in the 1950 World Cup, some British journalists back home reported the result as 10-1 to England! They couldn't believe the score-line and assumed it was a mistake.

I suppose every cloud has a silver lining. Those recurring England losses in the early 1950s eventually led to the lifting of the maximum wage for players in the Football League in 1961. They also accelerated the debate about the need to reward and prepare British players properly – pay them for what was their profession, the thing they did best, much better than you or me, their livelihood. The new pay deal suddenly meant that some rising young stars like George Best could – at least for a short while in his case – really live the high life.

SRC: The British footballing jean-genie was finally out of the box.

CHAPTER 2

Teams Of Eleven-A-Side

JW: Why does football have eleven players a side? Could we ever really know why? Eleven may sound like an arbitrary number, though with a lonely goalkeeper it does offer a bit of symmetry out on the pitch: five and five on each side of the field. It could also be something to do with the optimum number of players given the chosen pitch size. But it's probably something both more obvious and more complicated.

SRC: That other, rather boring, English game, that summer vision in white cricket, had eleven-a-side well before football took hold.

JW: Cricket is certainly the older sport and it did have eleven players a side – a balance of five batsmen and five bowlers, plus an extra player to keep wicket [cricket's goalkeeper] and to ensure that everyone had a chance to bat. Many early football teams were formed to keep cricketers fit during the winter. Sheffield and also Hallam FC, two of the world's first football clubs, grew up like this. Local men such as Nathaniel Creswick and William Prest in Sheffield helped produce its own local rules before the national FA laws were devised in 1863. But even these clubs out in the northern provinces were probably influenced, at some level, by public schoolboys returning to the sticks with a lofty vision of how to organize sports for the less privileged. The good men of Sheffield first drew up stumps and only when the dark nights set in did they take to kicking a football.

SRC: So, early football clubs in England were often reliant on your 'boring' old cricket to get started.

JW: When the early winter game eventually split into three different codes – association football, rugby league, and rugby union – this produced different numbers of players

A Second Division 'team of all the talents' - Sunderland had beaten Leeds United to win the English FA Cup, 1973.
(Mirrorpix)

for each code: eleven, thirteen, and fifteen, respectively. The handling split came in 1871, when the Rugby Football Union was formed. But the rugby men were themselves two tribes. The working-class league professionals, who were based in a corridor across the north of England, went their own way in 1895, with upper-class union amateurs dominating in other parts of the north and the south/west. Different again, Wales tried hardest to maintain rugby union as a sport for all classes. Both rugby codes wanted their version of football to be different from each other and their Association rival. So, they clutched their oval ball close to their chests and played the numbers game.

SRC: For me, eleven-a-side football is still *the* game; not five, or seven, or the nine-a-side stuff. Whilst I get it that fielding smaller football teams allows everyone to have a touch, I get irritated these days by all the formats and different numbers of players playing football. If it's not eleven, I instantly think it's not an important game. At school you may have had various configurations in the playground at lunchtime, but the honor always was to make 'the first eleven.' Okay, there are increasing numbers of subs allowed now, and it can get very tactical, but the maximum number of players you are allowed on the field is still the perfect eleven.

The England ex-manager Bobby Robson, from Stanley in County Durham, once said: 'If six of yours can play better than six of theirs, then you have a decent chance of winning.' Seven, and your chances are improved. Eight, and it's a forgone conclusion. Nine, and it's a case of try to keep count of the goals. Ten, and the other team might as well not bother turning up – it's hardly a match. So, we should stick to eleven players, just to ensure that (Sir) Bobby's slide rule to football success carries on working.

Jimmy Greaves, footballer, playing for the
Chelsea Cricket Eleven, summer 1958
(Mirrorpix)

JW: But a lot of other things have changed over time: how players train; certain laws; tactics and systems; the rise of managers and coaches. The offside law was revised way back in the 1920s to make the game more entertaining,

to get more goals. Even as TV has become much more demanding today and insisting on more entertainment for the armchair masses, nothing has shifted the game from eleven-a-side. So, it must work. No one seriously argues that because today's players are so much fitter and faster and do twice as much running as those baggy-shorted men of yesteryear, that we need fewer players on the pitch to make it exciting.

SRC: This means that once upon a time in football history the game was like an open book – anything could happen, anyone could play and kick a ball. Then gradually, in the name of Empire and around the factories up north and elysian green fields beneath Harrow School where Lord Byron attended – we get this national agreement on the number of players, on a common pitch size, on laws being introduced. It all goes mainstream.

JW: In 1888 local merchants and businessmen got twelve clubs to step up from the north and the midlands to form this new union of clubs, the Football League. Basically this was so that they could get the timing of fixtures set in stone and publicized for the coming season. It was a sign of the new modern age of clock-time, of paying fans, and of an emerging national press. Football supporters who paid for entry for matches now needed to know exactly where and when these would take place. Regular Saturday afternoon kickoffs meant that working men could get home from work, eat and get washed, and then walk or cycle to the match. The railway network meant fans could even get to some away matches. But it wasn't so easy to convince clubs to join the new league because no one could guarantee it would be successful.

And it did have its early teething problems. Players didn't always turn up to matches on time, so the pre-selected eleven sometimes didn't start. League officials also squabbled over details about exactly how clubs should be ranked at the season's end, even *after* the league had been launched. It was a chaotic beginning, but still rather more ordered and better organized than what had gone before.

SRC: Football, with a capital F, now had something to protect. I can see this was its first real leap in the dark. Yet once various leagues were launched and new clubs from all over joined up, football quickly became part of the national psyche.

Spurs manager Bill Nicholson and his players, following their victory over
Leicester City in the FA Cup final, clinching an historic double, 1960-61
(Mirrorpix)

League football has only seriously been interrupted twice, both times by war. What a thought: that only world wars could stop football, the sport which shaped the national sporting calendar for British people.

JW: Pretty much all the early senior professional football clubs in England and Wales were named after real places, so reading about or hearing the weekend results every winter Saturday somehow confirmed our national well-being. Football effectively became the sporting map of Britain. We even launched trawlers to go fishing, and then to war, named after football clubs. The HMS Notts County was requisitioned by the Admiralty in 1939 and was sunk by German U-boats in March 1942. The Notts County club lives on, of course though, for obvious reasons, its fans never liked talking about it 'going down' or 'sinking to the bottom' of the league table.

SRC: For a long time we believed we were in charge of the world game having bossed the seven seas with British sea power. But the game honed in the UK had already been exported. The cat was out of the bag.

In 1953 the Hungarians showed up and said: 'Okay,

give us your very best eleven. We'll show you how a *real* team do it.' The Magyars had been playing a very different kind of football to us, in which any man could do a 'drag-back' or fill in at any of the ten outfield positions given his all-round gifts. Hungary was the number-one team in the world at the time when they came to hallowed Wembley, where the confident home nation had never been beaten by foreign opposition. They destroyed England, 6-3. This was supposed to be our sacred turf at the heart of England, a land which saw off every threat of invasion. This defeat truly upset the English apple-cart.

JW: And it got worse: the next year England went out to Budapest, planning to avenge this defeat, only to get thrashed again, this time 7-1. The Scots also played this Hungary team home and away and lost both times. Communism triumphed – at football. It was the moment when the British game might have been jolted out of its complacency. Our island-nation was slowly awaking from the assumption that we would always be able to teach the rest of the world how to play football.

But this view was hard to shake, even though our clubs struggled in the new European tournaments. Our domestic competitions seemed like they had it all – and in a sense they did. In the fifties and sixties, small town clubs in England could still collect together the best eleven players they could muster and win titles and play in cup finals. Look at the success in the early 1960s of one of the founders of the Football League, modest Lancashire Burnley, reputedly the first club in the world to build a training ground rather than train in their home stadium. Burnley were Football League champions in 1960. Back then, wages were limited, contracts binding, and good players could be retained by the smaller clubs. Transfers and contracts were controlled by chairmen, not by players and agents. An occasional player escaped abroad, but very few British footballers wanted a move to improve their 'lifestyle.'

SRC: There's something quite heroic and more inclusive yelling at me from those photographs that mark this period, when austerity and the post-war gray began to show glimpses of color as the Instamatic camera became more available.

There's this rather humble way that teams of the day come across as 'we are all in it together.' And yet, these photos say very little about the individual journeys and

*West Ham United team, 1964, photographed at home, complete with unswept terraces. Bobby Moore, far right, went
on to captain England in their 1966 World Cup victory, whilst Geoff Hurst, fifth from right, scored a hat trick in the same game.*
(Mirrorpix)

hardships that players might have endured to make the team at that moment.

Pictures of Chelsea FC from that period carry a very personal message for me. When I was young, my family gave a temporary home every summer to various kids from London who didn't have much in life or much to say for themselves. But they did seem to light up at the mention of Chelsea FC and Stamford Bridge. So, I started to think that there was something very special about that blue Chelsea strip, and that beneath the Stamford Bridge flowed some very good water which could offer up fantastic football teams, a match for anyone.

JW: Because of these quirks in our past, acquaintances made, or a football ground we were taken to in our youth, it is quite easy to develop ties with another club, links that may be difficult to explain but that we just can't shake off.

SRC: Definitely my story. I am made in Watford, yet Chelsea – because of my London visitors' connection – is also part of my football DNA. Burnley and 1961 double-winning Spurs were the best two teams in the land when I was born, so I also have an elevated, retrospective respect for them.

A Hungarian I know has a Liverpool FC tattoo on her

'With A Splash Of Frenchman' - Leeds United, 1992
France's Eric Cantona lifting the English League championship trophy
(SRC)

back, all because in the sixties her Hungarian dad started looking to England (football and the Beatles) and its fab teams after his own Magical Magyars (one defeat in six years) got broken up in 1956. Bill Shankly was a native socialist who would have understood the importance of the Hungarian uprising.

JW: The public thirst for the British game in the 1950s was married to that postwar feeling of recovery – of austerity's days being numbered. The nation stepped forward together through its clamor for football, even though we all followed our different clubs. I thought

the *Charles Buchan Football Monthly* and then *Kenneth Wolstenholme's* Christmas annuals of the 1960s reflected a new sporting outlook: a message that we needed no more than *this* team of eleven keen, fit young men to succeed.

So far, these elevens had largely been made up of homegrown players. A handful – John Charles, Jimmy Greaves, Gerry Baker, Denis Law among them – went abroad to earn some decent money. But few British stars stayed away for very long and very few foreign players ever came to play in Britain. It was still a remarkably insular British game – each to their own.

The Hungary football team visit the Pathé News Studio in London to watch the film of their 6-3 demolition of England at Wembley Stadium the previous day, November 1953
(Mirrorpix)

SRC: But we had really good players in Britain in the sixties. The Scots were very strong and, fabulously – they are still heralded today – the West Ham United academy provided the backbone of the England World Cup winning team of '66. This vision of top-quality homegrown talent is confirmed by the picture on page 14 of the club's players lined up on the Upton Park terraces. No one had even bothered to clean 'the studio' and the saintly Bobby Moore is made to stand on an empty crisp packet. Donning shorter shorts than ever before, these players are surely a symbol of the youthful bravado and modernism of the time – showing more athletic flesh – not hiding behind anything.

JW: So, what do you think finally changed our ideas about our best eleven players being British, all playing for British clubs? How did we learn to do things differently?

SRC: Bobby Robson's Ipswich had imported stars – proven Dutch players – but I believe the punt taken on the introduction of an unknown Eric Cantona broke the English mold. Now the idea grew that clubs might tweak their team with the introduction of an *Eric* from abroad – a small risk taken and yet it could just work out.

Leeds United, who signed Cantona, had a core of top British players: Gary Speed, Gordon Strachan, David Batty. It transpired – sheer genius on the manager's part

– that all they needed to do was add into their mix a Gallic genius (at odds with his own country) and this would get them across the winning-line. Okay, he only played fifteen league games for Leeds in the run-in of the 1991-1992 season, but *CAN-TO-NA* added that extra *je ne sais quoi* at a crucial time. He had an even bigger effect at Manchester United when he moved there.

JW: Certainly, foreign talent has reached a near saturation level in the Premier League today (more like a World League, only one-third British players). This need to import talent may be a lesson we can indirectly trace back to those hammerings in the 1950s, by Ferenc Puskás and his Hungarian teammates.

SRC: All I can say is that my dad came home from Wembley in 1953 after *his* England had been thrashed by Hungary and, not normally a drinker, he knocked back a large gin and tonic before retiring straight to bed. From that time on he never took any foreign player or foreign team for granted. If his beloved Watford FC were drawn against some unknown (to him) Bulgarian side, say in the UEFA Cup, then that loss to Hungary always had him suspecting that we would fall short as a club and as a football nation. Talent was also *out there*.

FA Cup final lineup, cartoon, 1967
(Mirrorpix)

JW: We could be discussing an early Brexit and quotas for foreigners here. But I think we agree that competition against the very best and the inward flow of migrant talent to Britain has enriched the British club game, transforming our football ideas and our teams of homegrown eleven-a-sides, much for the better.

Has it improved the national team? Debatable.

CHAPTER 3

Manager Needed

'Herbert Chapman Statue' - Arsenal, 2014
(SRC)

SRC: So, we eventually learned that eleven homegrown players may not, in and of themselves, be enough to build great football sides. Or even good ones.

But there's another actor in all this. He was never part of the first eleven (as if it was ever all down to them). We also developed in Britain the cult of the manager, a man who is often held up today as almost equal to the input of the entire team.

JW: Opinions about managers dominate football talk today, but most early football clubs in Britain got by without what we would recognize now as a football manager. They had a secretary, someone who looked after the players (and the general running of the club) during the week, and a trainer – a fitness man – who made sure that the players were fit and ready to play. But it was the board, the directors, who usually picked the team at most clubs. And club directors did most of the scouting and made decisions on who to sign and how much to pay. The football manager only really became widely

recognized in Britain from the mid-1950s. An exception was the Yorkshireman Herbert Chapman, who back in the 1920s and 1930s became *the* first great football Svengali in Britain. He was a true visionary, a man way ahead of his time.

SRC: His statue outside the Emirates is impressive. But then Chapman, the son of a coal-miner, was a very remarkable man. He took an unfashionable northern club Huddersfield Town and managed them out of mediocrity to *three* consecutive league titles – champions of all England.

JW: And then, blow the house down, he went south to sophisticated Arsenal and did the same with them. In fact, he brought the very first league championship to the south. Yes, it took until 1931, forty-three years after the Football League had been formed, for the south of England to catch up with the industrial north. What kept them? Southern clubs not joining the early Football

'Manager Up In The Air - Sean Dyche' - Burnley, 2014
(SRC)

Brian Clough, then a player for Sunderland FC,
at home with his record collection, January 1964
(Mirrorpix)

had some managerial greats. Jock Stein, Bill Nicholson, Matt Busby, Don Revie, and the incomparable Bill Shankly, a man who, while manager at Carlisle United and then Grimsby Town, introduced a public-address system (he always liked to talk). He even embarrassed one of the Town eleven over the tannoy one day by talking publicly about the player's domestic strife. Shankly wanted his clubs to 'come home' to the fans. In Liverpool he could turn up, unannounced, at supporters' funerals.

JW: Football crowds were falling in the sixties, precisely because there were other options in life – other things to do – like spending more time in your house, watching TV or playing the latest Frank Sinatra disc on your Dansette record player!

SRC: In the *football coming of age in the modern period* 1960s, I guess it was an opinionated joker, Brian Clough, who best symbolized the brash, new version of the young football manager for the television age. When he got seriously injured in 1962, Clough took on added responsibility by going into management. He was only thirty. Soon he became a TV voice, a personality, as much as a football boss. People say they tuned in to watch the football highlights but really to hear the bone-dry Clough's opinions.

JW: The British press was becoming increasingly interested in celebrity lives beyond the football ground – the lifestyles of players and managers alike. Big names overseeing the game were almost expected to have big egos, and TV was the populist arena in which to spin them out. Alex Ferguson, another former player with a truncated career and strong views, appeared to be a one-off, but he actually came from a great line of exceptional and knowledgeable Scottish football managers.

SRC: But where are the great English football managers now?

JW: In the 1960s, homegrown successful British managers were tough cookies, men who could bring all the necessary ingredients together to forge a winning team. At that time, Scottish and northeast mining communities appeared to be like a sporting blast furnace for producing the ideal managerial mold. Some committed Scottish bosses – like the genius Jock Stein – even died on the job.

League was obviously a barrier. Herbert Chapman was certainly much more than a great coach: he took complete charge of the football and marketing side at Arsenal, unusual for its day. *(I wonder if Arsène will get a statue, too?)*

Chapman not only built great sides at two very different clubs, north and south, but he understood tactics, negotiated smart deals, mastered man management, and promoted great teamwork. He fostered revolutionary ideas about how the game could appeal more to its supporters and he recognized, even then, the importance of the media. He wanted TV coverage, floodlights, white footballs, numbers on shirts, and distinctive kits, well before these became fashionable. Arsenal's world-famous outfit of red with white sleeves was invented by Chapman, in 1933. Funnily enough, it was almost the same strip adopted in 1947 by the club in the town of his birth, Rotherham United.

SRC: Between then and the Premier League era, we have

Brian Clough, manager at thirty-one years of age, with his Derby County team, October 1967
(Mirrorpix)

The last *English* manager to win the league title was Howard Wilkinson, at Leeds United, and that was even before the Premier League was formed. Perhaps we do have a thing here for *nearly* men. Sir Bobby Robson was a partial exception but even he was more noted for his management career abroad. He became a national treasure, of course, but mainly perhaps for being an honorable man more than a really great manager.

Most people would say today that someone like Sean Dyche has done a very decent job as a top-level English football manager. But no one would say he's a Bobby Robson, never mind a Clough, a Bill Shankly, or a Fergie.

SRC: It's clear that at the very top level the impact of a great manager can make the difference. In the late nineties, Arsène Wenger changed both Arsenal and the entire English game. But lower down the ladder? Do smaller clubs need managers at all?

JW: Most of those successful guys in the second, third, and fourth tiers tend to be grounded and humble – just an extension of the team really. Most of the old northern players who went on to become good managers were saved from manual jobs, in the pits and factories, saved by a better life in football. So, these are not people who are necessarily sent by God; they're shift managers who just have to work with what they've got and try to make a silk purse out of not very much.

Before the Premier League came along, most top players only really respected other men who had played the game and had a decent career: the 'one-of-us' hand-me-downs. These days, other routes have opened up –

Players Alex Ferguson and Bert Paton exercising
for Dunfermline Athletic, March 1966
(Mirrorpix)

Jock Stein, manager of Scotland, stumbles and collapses, watched by
assistant manager Alex Ferguson at the end of Wales v Scotland
match at Ninian Park in Cardiff, 1985
(Mirrorpix)

in various forms of coaching and management - as elite football has become more analytical, more reliant on research and on devising new 'scientific' systems of play.

It's a brainier business today. Now there is more chance that you can make players believe in you if you can show them that you have seen the data, understand the game, and can control a group of anxious, ambitious egos. You no longer have to have served in the trenches to be trusted in the dressing room.

SRC: And yet, all managers in the end (like politicians) suffer the same fate - except maybe for Arsène Wenger and Sir Alex Ferguson. It drives people like me to distraction that the tenure of managers today seems to get shorter and shorter, and still we talk more and more about replacing them. 'Six defeats in a row and you're sacked' has become an accepted algorithm.

Sometimes, when the tabloids and radio talk shows bore on and on about sacking a manager and the public gets sucked into the debate, I wish we could just get rid of managers entirely. Let teams run themselves and prove their worth or collapse trying.

JW: Think on. Without Graham Taylor, your very own club Watford FC would have been very average in the 1980s. He changed the club from top to bottom - or bottom to top. I don't think we would want to pass up the opportunity of having really special football managers moving among our men. I don't even think that we could get by easily without a group of more standard managers - certainly the board can't do it, the fans can't do it, and the players need a guide, and someone to blame when things go wrong.

Like it or not, managers ARE needed.

CHAPTER 4

Who Owns The Club?

JW: So, it's heaven's will that:
1. *Good managers can build a great team.*
2. *They don't have to be British (these days).*
3. *They CAN turn a struggling club around –*
   if they are a Graham Taylor.

But there is a group of people above them: financiers, actors, wheeler-dealers, some genuinely capable people, who we can't ignore. These are the men behind the scenes who run and own football clubs – or think they do.

SRC: I like the story of a local man, Jack Walker, buying a very traditional football club in Blackburn Rovers in the 1990s, arriving in a standard saloon car with his mates outside Ewood Park, rolling up his sleeves and saying: 'Well, I can bring something to this party. I've got some money, I know what to do.' Jack's the local maverick figure: 'Job to do, better be getting on with it' mentality. Walker's business background was steel, but he could have been a (rich) plumber one supposes. He never took his eye off the ball and then when his chance came along…

JW: A rover's return. But what exactly do owners bring to the party? Is it payback time? Once upon a time people like you and I might have believed in a local guy who put his money and time into the club and we probably would have presumed he was doing a good job for the local community. But things have changed. Whilst managers could only get a job in a club if they had some sort of football pedigree, owners just needed hard cash, some business acumen, possibly some bluster. Two out of three would usually do it.

SRC: In the 1960s, when football fans were beginning to choose their own lifestyles and preferences, doubts about owners were already stirring: 'Hold on – my father and his

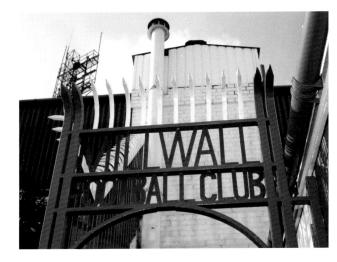

'Entrance To The Old Den' - Millwall, 1991
(SRC)

father watched this club. Don't mess it up.' And by the 2000s this view was keener still: 'You can't waltz in now and start talking about owning our club, just because you have money.'

People have started cultivating, collecting, and valuing the history of their football clubs – almost any club in the land – and are even keeping an eye on other clubs that are not their own. They get indignant over the mistreatment of fellow supporters. Because of generations of support handed down, they think themselves to be, somehow, the real custodians of their clubs, seeing the whole football landscape as some kind of elaborate family-history puzzle.

JW: That's the romantic version. But try telling that to the people – whatever you might say about them – who have legally bought the club with real money and have done all the paperwork to say it's *theirs*.

SRC: Blackburn-born Jack Walker back in 1991, flush

'The Arrival Of Jack Walker' - Blackburn Rovers, 1992
(SRC)

with £360 million from selling his Walkersteel company, is definitely different from the owners who followed him later in the post-1992 Premier League era. Assem Allam, the British-Egyptian owner of a Rolls-Royce and Hull City FC, in his public statements, makes his motives *sound* like Jack Walker's: an obligation to pay back the region for his own success. But whilst Jack wanted his Rovers to return to being the successful club of his youth, Assem took over Hull City in 2010 and wanted change for the future. Naively perhaps, he had visions of furry tigers selling well in the Far East and making his club more marketable worldwide as Hull City Tigers. Jack Walker's ambitions were much more local.

Sucked along in the global Premier League boom (and Hull City had got there for the first time), AA thought little of trying to switch the club's name – overturning 100 years of tradition – all part of a day or two in the office considering the marketing and modernization of Hull City. *The fans turned against him.* Roared against him in fact. At most clubs, if not at Rovers and Hull City, what the fans collectively pay at the turnstile, on pre-match ticket sales, and in buying extras like shirts and merchandise, still exceeds the cash put in or loaned by the 'owner.'

JW: A postmodern, global football tale. In the past, football clubs introduced local business people into some

'The Chairman And His Prize' - Hull City, 2013
(SRC)

very powerful and influential networks. Imagine, too, the income you might conjure directly from football if you were, say, a lawyer, a brewer, a pie-maker, or a builder. Over time, football fans pretty much forgot who owned their clubs. Owners in the 1980s wanted no public profile. People on the board were generally a bit boring, aside from Watford's celebrity chairman Elton John, a glitzy exception.

The reality is that most football clubs lost money – most still do. Keeping a local club alive in hard times was what supporters relied on local club owners and directors to manage. Football clubs have gone bust, of course, but few of them disappear.

Directors rolled up to the club AGM every year, listened to a few disgruntled voices, and then set about the new season running it much as before. But probably nothing like the way they ran their own businesses. Football was a weekend hobby with a few more cigars thrown in and they faced little opposition. The fanzine culture of the 1980s

did, however, stir things up a little. Fans have had to learn much more since about football business.

SRC: Some clubs, like Millwall in London for example, an intensely working-class outfit, seem to feel that they can never really be 'owned' at all because they're just such a spiky club. If the Lord Himself came down to walk through those formidable gates to reorganize the embattled Den stadium, Millwall fans would probably say: 'Sorry guv'nor, hands off. This is *our* club.' Millwall fans – and there are one or two other examples, neighbors West Ham United, for one – seem bent on 'owning' their club in the sort of muscular way that just isn't in the character of many other football places.

JW: Yes, West Ham supporters have certainly been annoyed by owners who levered the club out of their loved home and then promised the moon. Take another case, well-meaning Vincent Tan chairman at Cardiff City in

South Wales. Here is an owner with his own revolutionary ideas: change the club's historic colors from blue to red to make Cardiff City the national club of Wales. Science had also told him that red was the proven color of winners. Which is actually not so crazy because the great physicist Stephen Hawking also argued that science proved that playing in red and in a 4-3-3 outfield formation held the best prospect for football success. Hawking also devised a formula for taking penalty kicks: high shots by bald, fair-haired players were the best bet. Who knew?

Tan, however, failed miserably to win Cardiff supporters over and, science or no science, their fans soon kicked his revolutionary crystal ball clean over the popular stand.

SRC: The American Glazer family bought Manchester United in 2005 and also borrowed money against the football business to clinch the deal. United had some success but also lost hundreds of millions of pounds in interest charges and dividends to the owners and their family.

Some United radicals decided to go back to their roots with a new club, FC United of Manchester, because they were enraged by the Americanization of a great English club. They felt manipulated by owners from thousands of miles away. FC United's mantra is: 'We are the club, the club is us. We are not for profit. We own defeat, we own failure. We can't walk away.' Success for FC United is making ends meet and having a good time while raising a standard. FC United aims to maintain a set of values which they believed had gone AWOL at corporatized Manchester United. The red heart is their flag, not the dollar sign.

JW: Even FCUM have had their recent upheavals. We live in new times. For most of the history of the English game, making money from football was really not that easy, but today foreign investors are falling over each other to milk what looks like a Premier League cash cow.

Spending money in English football also buys you soft power: the Chinese, the people from Qatar, the Manchester Sheiks, Roman Abramovich at Chelsea. Who's next? Who is richer still? These are the kind of people – and governments – who have so much money they can get bored by their own vast wealth. What to do with all that cash? What looks interesting and has influence? What are people talking about? Where can I meet other super-

powerful people, like me? The Premier League ticks a lot of these boxes. It's a playpen for the global uber rich.

SRC: It's a kind of bling checklist, isn't it? Buy a massive yacht! Tick. Buy *one, two, three, four, five, six*, at least *seven* houses in the most magnificent locations in the world. Tick. Buy my partner whatever he, or she, wants. Tick. Give away a few of your global businesses for the kids to play with. Tick. And then people start to ask you: 'Why haven't you bought a Premier League football club?' This new set of uber-rich global club owners may not always be in football for the good of the game.

JW: But when a club is in real trouble, or just ambitious for change, even die-hard fans can sometimes close their eyes and cross their fingers. Supporters' groups, which may have spent years wrestling the club back from reckless owners or from possible extinction, can sometimes give in to the easier path of a rich benefactor. And so, the crazy cycle goes on. In the end – and even at the lower levels of the game – more money will always be needed. Expectations become inflated.

'Simple Pure Love Affair' - FC United, 2015
(SRC)

SRC: It's also true that, faced with a vacuum - standing still, or a potential investor who pulls out - there might even be a reluctant acceptance of the return of the old maligned board: to men who had a few bob between them, didn't give up, but rather watched from the wings or from behind the curtains as it all went pear-shaped. Then, like the *Thunderbirds*, they are back in for the unlikely international rescue. It happened at my own local club,

'The Chairman's Dream Of Too Much On His Plate' - Carlisle United, 1993
(SRC)

Carlisle United. Owners often want their cake – and other people's cake as well – and want to scoff the lot.

JW: There are still some good people around, owners from home and abroad, people who want the very best for their clubs and for the fans who support them. Like Steve Gibson at Middlesbrough, who has pumped money in and stuck by his hometown club. And fans have also sensibly stepped in – heroically in some cases – to rescue some smaller clubs that may have flown too close to the sun or been duped by impostors.

SRC: In fact, the more I think about it, it's patently clear what people like Jack Walker at Blackburn Rovers were all about. As the owner of local businesses employing half the town, Jack saved up everyone else's money and then gave a good deal of it back – he reinvested it in the local football club. And because this took bigger clubs by surprise, he even carried his unfashionable town to the Premier League title in 1995.

JW: More than that, he did all of this on the site of Ewood Park, where almost the entire Rovers story had been played out since the club helped found the Football League back in 1888. He expanded and modernized the stadium, of course, but it is still surrounded by those familiar neighborhood streets, nineteenth-century houses where the club's earliest players and their families once lived.

SRC: 'The house that the locally raised Jack built' raises

another dynamic – if you happen to come from afar to buy an English football club in an age when television is king, why do you need to keep it in the same place it has always been? Why does Ewood Park, or Deepdale at Preston North End, or 'home' matter at all in these increasingly placeless times? There was that string of American-style adverts, which talked about moving Arsenal to the rural Peak District in Derbyshire where there was a bit more space for development. Not so far off someone else's truth.

Arsenal, when they moved from the Highbury Stadium to not far away, at least tried to preserve the memory and integrity of their hemmed-in, once-great ground. They turned their glorious turf into a park and some of the stands became (expensive) homes. People could still 'worship' there and walk the dog. It should always be the responsibility of the owner or caretaker in selling off any football ground to make sure it becomes a place of pilgrimage. Take Roker Park in Sunderland: over the course of its lifetime it has hosted literally millions of people having the time of their lives through football. How can it possibly be that when time was finally called on this historic venue they simply knocked it down, flattened it; abused its memory? They sold it off for a few medium-quality houses. The developers' only concession was to label roads within the new estate with English football references: Turnstile Mews, Midfield Drive, Promotion Close, etc. This is quite pathetic. Would one have knocked down a church with so little care? Who is this supposed to benefit? There were, and are still, loads of scruffy bits of land just a stone's throw away from the old Roker Park which could have been built on. It's as if someone - a force from within even - wants to do down the very things we most hold dear. It feels like a local form of self-harm but on a national scale, because there are numerous equivalents of Roker Park. Let's hope the same fate does not await historic Goodison Park in the city of Liverpool. These are sacred places, where we have most felt at home.

JW: And pity the fans of those league clubs today that cannot be sure of a home at all. In February 2019, Coventry City in Shakespeare country were given just two months by the Football League to find a stadium in which they could play their home fixtures in 2019/20. City's hedge fund proprietors had no agreement in place with the Ricoh Stadium owners Wasps, a Premiership Rugby club. Here was a great football club, potentially homeless in 2020. How did we get here?

CHAPTER 5

Playing At Home

'Big Open Discussion' - Barnsley, Yorkshire, 2014
(SRC)

SRC: The idea of home for me is of an immovable object: it's a material thing of course, but it is also an identity and a sense of place. Home is where most of us want to be at Xmas – with our families – and home in a football sense is just an extension of this. A site where your forefathers and mothers also trod. It has a history. It's yours to decorate.

JW: Home has a very special meaning in football, of course: we speak a lot about 'playing at home' and being 'drawn at home' and 'home advantage.' It certainly seems to make a major difference to results. The statistics say that, on average, home teams win more than half their games whilst away teams only win one quarter. That's quite a split. Referees can be swayed by a home crowd. And clubs can have problems switching homes – check out the recent West Ham situation. How is it that a stadium and its fans can mean so much?

SRC: It doesn't add up. Even if you play a match at home

with no fans (behind closed doors), it's still an advantage. Maybe the ghosts of home supporters are cheering you on?

Most football fans have a central message. No matter how shambolic you might think our ground is, we really LOVE this place. Most football grounds were not set up to be especially beautiful palaces, but they were always a safe space for locals. A spiritual place. A place of pilgrimage. An altar, of sorts.

We won't go on here about football as a substitute for religion, but a stadium *is* a kind of sacred gathering ground, a destination, an Oz at the end of the rainbow. Just as Glastonbury in England, the home of a giant annual music festival, has come to signify much more than an ancient religious center, a football ground is active and earthquakes of the human spirit regularly happen there too.

JW: 'Earthquakes of the human spirit' is a wonderful phrase. The home football ground is not just about bricks and concrete; that's clear. It is much more about what the stadium *means* to local people: a beautifully painted wall, or some familiar and friendly girders can carry all kinds of messages and comfort, missed by most of us. But it is also about how aspects of that meaning can make it an oppressive and threatening place for visitors, the enemy. Being an away fan is enjoyable – the trip and all that invasive singing and chanting – but it's also a kind of intrusion. Sometimes, you can feel like an unwelcome and a very unappreciated guest in the away end. And each football club has its own message for visitors, encoded in its stadium. There is a kind of siege mentality thing which goes on around 'our' home patch. Only when something huge that affects us all occurs – like a Hillsborough, for example – can football fans easily pull together and share a truly collective identity and the associated pain.

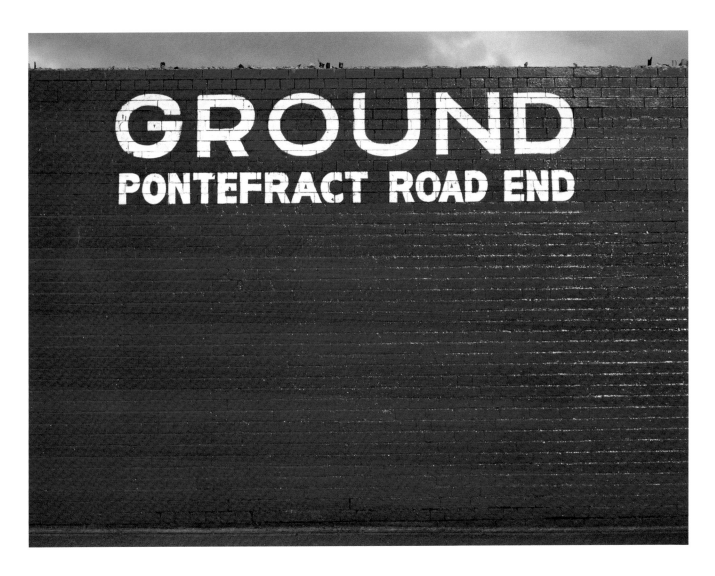

'Blood Red Road End' - Barnsley, 1993
(SRC)

SRC: The Hillsborough disaster in 1989 was obviously a key moment, a time when we had to reflect on what we valued about our existing homes and what urgently needed to change. Some of those favorite nooks and crannies, which defined our homes – which made them ours – would now have to go. Could we hold on to the soul of our football grounds?

JW: We could all see, I think, that Lord Justice Taylor's inquiry pronouncements in 1990 after Hillsborough were going to produce a new football stadium experience; a much bigger shift than the impact of player transfers, or even the new TV deals. They were going to change our very homes. Some of us might have complained in the past about poor facilities, terrible toilets, or even difficulties in seeing the match in some grounds. We may have wanted to wash our hands of some of the old eyesores, but we were still pretty clear-eyed about keeping all existing Football League clubs and defending their homes. Non-fans must have wondered why.

SRC: What distinguishes this country is that there are SO MANY clubs and identities closely packed together. We value them all as part of the national football story.

'Green And Pleasant Football Land,' 2020

© By Stuart Roy Clarke and Stuart Beveridge

UNST
BALTASOUND
WHALSAY
HARBISON
PARK

THURSO
THE VIKINGS

HALKIRK UNITED
RECREATION PARK
THE ANGLERS

DURNESS

WICK ACADEMY
THE SCORRIES
HARMSWORTH
GOLSPIE PARK
SUTHERLAND
KING GEORGE
V PARK

CARLOWAY
COCK
CHOLICH
STORNOWAY
UNITED
ATHLETIC
NESS
FIVEPENNY
BACK

LOCHBROOM
DUDGEON PARK
RANGERS
BRORA
RANGERS
THE CATTACHS
BALINTORE
SEABOARD
PARK

ALNESS
UNITED
DALMORE
THE STAGGIES
PARK VICTORIA
ROSS COUNTY
PARK
INVERNESS CITY GRANT STREET
NORTHERN MEETING PARK

LOSSIEMOUTH
THE COASTERS
GRANT PARK
FORRES MECHANICS
MOSSET PARK
THE CAN CANS

BUCKIE THISTLE
THE JAGS
VICTORIA PARK
KEITH
KYNOCH PARK
THE MAROONS

FRASERBURGH
THE BROCH
BELLSLEA PARK
PETERHEAD
BALMOOR
THE BLUE TOON
TURRIFF UNITED
THE HAUGHS
FORMARTINE UNITED
NORTH LODGE PARK

BENBECULA

UIG
SKYE
SPORTREE
KYLEAKIN

STAFFIN

INVERNESS
CALEDONIAN
THISTLE
STATION PARK
NAIRN
COUNTY
"SUPER CALEY GO
BALLISTIC CELTIC
ARE ATROCIOUS"

ELGIN CITY
BOROUGH
BRIGGS
DUFFTOWN
THE TOONSERS

HUNTLY
CHRISTIE PARK
BLACK AND GOLDS
COVE RANGERS
HIGHLAND
DYNAMITE
ALLAN PARK

PLOCKTON

STRATHSPEY
THISTLE
SEAFIELD PARK

FORT
WILLIAM
CLAGGAN
PARK
BLANEFIELD
THISTLE

INVERURIE LOCO WORKS
THE LOCIES HARLAW PARK
CROMBIE PARK
CULTER

ABERDEEN
PITTODRIE
THE DONS

MONTROSE
LINKS PARK
THE GABLE
ENDIES

OBAN SAINTS
GLENCRUITTEN PARK

VALE OF ATHOLL
"COME AWAY THE VALE"
THE HEDGEMEN
BRECHIN CITY
BLAIRGOWRIE JUNIOR
GLEBE PARK
THE BERRYPICKERS
SUNNYBANK
HEATHRYFOLD PARK
BANKS O' DEE
SPAIN PARK

ARBROATH
GAYFIELD
PARK
THE RED
LICHTIES

GREENOCK
MORTON
CAPPIELOW
PARK
THE PRIDE
OF CLYDE

DUNDOON
DAVIE PARK
DUNBLANE
THISTLE
ST. JOHNSTONE
McDIARMID
PARK
LETHAM

DENS PARK
THE DEE
DUNDEE
FORFAR ATHLETIC
THE LOONS
STATION PARK
DUNDEE UNITED
TANNADICE PARK
THE TERRORS

CLYDEBANK
THE BANKIES
HOLM PARK
CALLANDER
THISTLE
SEVEN ACRES PARK
THE TANGERINES
EAST FIFE
BAYVIEW
STADIUM

CARRADALE

LOCHGILPHEAD
RED STAR

GLASGOW CITY
PETERSHILL PARK
RANGERS
IBROX
GERS
FIRHILL
STADIUM
PARTICK
THISTLE
THE JAGS

STIRLING
ALBION
FORTHBANK
STADIUM

LOCHILVIEW PARK
STENHOUSEMUIR
THE WASPS

RAITH
ROVERS
STARK'S
PARK

QUEEN'S
PARK
HAMPDEN
PARK
CELTIC
THE BHOYS
CELTIC PARK

CAMELON JUNIORS
THE MARINERS
CARMUIRS PARK

FALKIRK
THE BAIRNS

COWDENBEATH
CENTRAL PARK
DUNFERMLINE
ATHLETIC
THE BLUE BRAZIL
EAST END PARK
THE PARS

BURNTISLAND
SHIPYARD

KILMARNOCK
RUGBY PARK
HAMILTON
ACADEMICAL
DOUGLAS
PARK

MOTHERWELL
THE STEELMEN
FIR PARK

ALBION
ROVERS

AIRDRIEONIANS
NEW BROOMFIELD
DIAMONDS

HIBERNIAN
HIBEES
EASTER
ROAD

AUCHINLECK
TALBOT
BEECHWOOD
PARK
GIRVAN
THE SEASIDERS

GLENBUCK
CHERRYPICKERS
BURNSIDE

LIVINGSTON
ALMONDVALE
THE LIONS

HEART OF MIDLOTHIAN
HEARTS HEARTS
GLORIOUS
HEARTS
TYNECASTLE

BERWICK
RANGERS
SHIELFIELD
PARK

AYR UNITED
SOMERSET PARK
THE HONEST MEN

CUMNOCK
JUNIORS
TOWNHEAD
PARK

GLENAFTON
ATHLETIC
LOCH PARK

GRETNA
RAYDALE PARK

ALNWICK
TOWN
THE COLLIERS
WOODHORN LANE
ASHINGTON

STRANRAER
STAIR PARK

QUEEN OF
THE SOUTH
PALMERSTON PARK
DOONHAMERS

ANNAN
ATHLETIC
GALABANK

THE ANVILS

CARLISLE
SHEEPMOUNT
CARLISLE
UNITED
BRUNTON PARK

MORPETH
TOWN
DOCTOR PIT WELFARE PARK
NORTH SHIELDS
BEDLINGTON TERRIERS
THE MORGUE

NEWCASTLE UNITED
ST JAMES PARK
"TOON ARMY TOON ARMY"

LINFIELD
THE BLUES
WINDSOR
PARK

CRUSADERS
SEAVIEW
THE HATCHETMEN
CLIFTONVILLE
SOLITUDE
THE REDS

SKY BLUES
BALLYMENA
UNITED
GLENAVON
MOURNEVIEW PARK
THE BRIDESMAIDS

LISBURN
DISTILLERY
THE WHITES
NEW GROSVENOR
STADIUM

WORKINGTON
BOROUGH PARK

BARROW
HOLKER STREET
BLUE BIRDS
BRAITHWAITE
AMBLESIDE
UNITED
ULLSWATER

SUNDERLAND
STADIUM OF LIGHT
BLACK CATS
SUNDERLAND RCA
MEADOW PARK

COLERAINE
BANNSIDERS
THE SHOWGROUNDS
DERRY CITY
BRANDYWELL
STADIUM
CANDYSTRIPES

GLENTORAN
THE COCK N HENS
NEWRY CITY
THE TOWN
SHOWGROUNDS
THE OVAL

MORECAMBE
THE SHRIMPS
GLOBE
ARENA
WINDERMERE
KENDAL
TOWN
CONISTON
KIRBY STEPHEN

SPENNYMOOR TOWN

HARTLEPOOL
UNITED
MONKEY
HANGERS
VICTORIA PARK

ST. GEORGES
LANCASTER CITY
GIANT AXE
BLACKPOOL
ROVERS
KENDAL
TOWN
PARKSIDE
MIDDLESBROUGH
RIVERSIDE
THE DOLLY BLUES
THE TWO BLUES
HERITAGE PARK
BISHOP AUCKLAND
ACCRINGTON

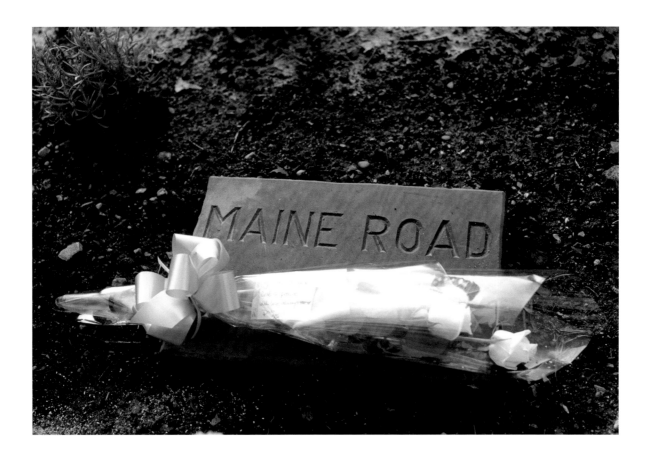

'Maine Road Was Where It Was At' - Manchester City, 2011
(SRC)

Americans, Germans, Scandinavians and others look on in amazement at this. A dozen Norwegians arrive at Grimsby Town's Blundell Park on the east coast of England from across the North Sea (not in Viking boats, I might add) and they are soon taking group selfies against the plain old terraced houses neighboring the ground.

Visitors are fascinated by all this historic detail we have around our football places. Not everything is perfectly arranged in the national football grid, of course; it's all a bit higgledy-piggledy. It's like a mad jigsaw – where is the plan? There may not have been one; football just sort of happened in this way, it took root around the nation. The locals feel honored, of course, that visiting Norwegians want to photograph their old houses – they even sweep the front step.

I am sure stadiums – our homes – that were sited in densely peopled areas, rather than plonked like a business unit in an industrial estate, speak to us much more as fans. When Manchester City moved across the city from Maine Road to the Etihad in 2003, the club instinctively knew that they had to take something of the old ground, their old home, with them. The Maine Road stone is a memorial to the former place and its people. It's repositioned today outside one of the posh entrances at the Etihad and is possibly the single-most photographed bit of the new ground.

I must say I am cheered by the fact that the British were shown at this moment to care very deeply about our football culture.

JW: Collectively we cried at the Hillsborough disaster and the events of 1989 and collectively we responded to what Lord Justice Taylor said in his inquiry report, and with some spirit of togetherness we rolled out the red carpet for the game's return, possibly to a new golden period. We prioritized it and got the thing rebuilt not quite overnight but over a few years and moreover – *with some care and with some love.*

CHAPTER 6

Fans Needed

West Ham fans queue at Upton Park as tickets for their FA Cup match
against Fulham go on sale, February 1958
(Mirrorpix)

'Forest Crowd Up Against It' - **Nottingham Forest at Aston Villa, 1991**
(SRC)

SRC: So we've got the whole picture of football now. You forget your hands, kick a ball around, call yourself a player, form yourself into teams of eleven, get yourself managed, find somewhere to call home, with a built-in home advantage. What else do we need?

FANS, of course, ideally recruited through ties of family and of place. Or through success – people from all over Britain became Nottingham Forest fans in the late 1970s because of what the manager Brian Clough achieved there.

Leeds United fans of a certain age also turn up today in the most unlikely of places. Or perhaps some of us

become football fans because we feel an underdog club will one day have its place in the sun? Peculiarly, we do consciously seem to follow clubs just because they are a bit useless – perhaps further proof of our masochism and loyalty. We, the British, love a good loser.

But where did early fans come from?

JW: In the past, those residents who lived around football grounds were an important part of a club's target audience. We have seen that British football clubs were usually set up in reasonably affluent working-class areas, so that working men with a bit of money to spend could

'Semifinal Crowd' - **West Ham United at Aston Villa, 1991**
(SRC)

walk to the match after work on Saturday mornings. There was public transport for others – buses and trams – though supporters arriving on bikes could often park them in local gardens for a small consideration. Clubs often rented terraced houses around grounds to staff, which was useful for postwar players because most of them didn't own cars.

The picture of London fans in the 1950s queuing in a quiet and orderly fashion is not even taken on a match-day. It's a daytime ticket collection for a fifth-round West Ham versus Fulham FA Cup tie. At least some of these people must have taken time out from work. Bosses would probably have worked out that some of their employees

will have slipped out of the depot, or office, for a couple of hours ticket queuing. Secret approval perhaps? This was, after all, a big deal locally – the magic of the FA Cup and a local derby match to boot.

SRC: What do people say: that the British are 'good' at queuing in a way, say, the Italians are not? (Is there a World Cup for queuing? The British would be clear favorites.) The British also love a good conga, which is a bit of queuing with an obvious inability to dance thrown in.

This picture also reminds me of images of queues for wartime food rationing in Europe. Most of the people here

Manchester United fans celebrate promotion back to the top flight,
at Notts County after a 2-2 draw, 1975
(Mirrorpix)

FA Cup Semifinal match at Hillsborough,
Nottingham Forest v Aston Villa, March 14, 1959
(Mirrorpix)

would have had memories of those austere days from only a decade before. British people had learned to bide their time: to sit out air raids calmly, to queue patiently. And, of course, to let the nice photographer take their picture.

In summary: the sort of people going to football in 1958 are the queuing sort. And they expect to have their photograph taken by the 'family' photographer.

JW: There are quite a few female faces in the front of this crowd. Some people might be surprised, but women have always watched the game, perhaps especially on these grand local occasions. Or are some of these women queuing on behalf of someone else, perhaps?

SRC: Over time, the overwhelming maleness of the game in Britain may have been taken for granted. Football can be a hive of pushing and shoving and blokes yelling. Sometimes it's assumed that the stadium is an arena where men can be men, can test you out or pin you with a look.

The man staring straight at me at Ipswich Town [page 36], at the end of an East Anglian 'Old Farm derby' with Norwich City, took me a little by surprise. I'd already met some Town fans wearing weird animal heads in the bar beneath the stand before the match. Out on the street, managing the crowds and scanning for possible trouble, the police had earlier been confronted by packs of (mainly) friendly lions, tigers, and bears. Then, in the stands whilst rival fans were still busy taunting each other, frustrated

at the inconclusive drawn outcome and wanting a bit of 'afters,' this tough-looking middle-aged guy stood out. Who in heavens had I met? I still took the photo, but it's not often that I have a 'stare-off' quite like this one. Usually, I try to make sure that my football pictures are quite natural and well observed. I had also almost forgotten about the book *Skinhead*. It had so left such an impression on me as a boy with its tales of violence and sex and football. And here it was again, a reminder on a T-shirt.

JW: Chaos all around him, this supporter seems completely stilled, doesn't he, caught in the eye of the storm. David Bowie said it best: 'When you are a boy, other boys check you out.' Older boys too.

SRC: All this looks so different from the exceptional 1959 photograph of Nottingham Forest fans at an FA Cup semifinal at Hillsborough. These supporters so wanted their team to do it in the [Manager Billy] 'Walker Way.' Forest did it, winning 1-0, but there is not much sense of the excited football carnival here.

Then, look at my pictures more than a generation later, of rival Nottingham Forest and West Ham United fans at another FA Cup semifinal, this time at Villa Park in 1991.

JW: That West Ham picture from 1991 could easily be from the 1950s: it's a very calm-looking crowd, expectant but also transfixed by your camera. The guy with the overgrown rosette looks timeless. In between those two moments of calm, thirty-two years apart, we know that things had actually grown much uglier in the British game.

Hooliganism really started to take off in England in the late 1960s, and when Manchester United got relegated in 1974 some of their younger supporters started targeting Second Division clubs, which were even less prepared to cope with the coming onslaught. By now, rival fans in England were divided by steel fences. It's now the 'psycho way' for Forest. And yet, if one took away the fences, they do look quite similar sorts of football gatherings, no? Only time – and fences – separate us.

There is a picture here of a typical Manchester United 'Red Army' trip to Notts County in 1975. A crush barrier seems to have been flattened in a celebratory melee. A solitary policeman looks on. It is an eerie signal of what lay ahead for the English game – serious crowd trouble and future stadium disasters.

'Queue For A Lancashire Away Day' - **Blackpool at Burnley, 1998**
(SRC)

SRC: I remember this period. When United fans came to town, businesses closed down and local residents boarded up their windows. For a while, hosting football in some places in Britain became like preparing for a visit from a hostile military unit.

If we compare this image from 1975 with one of my pictures from 1998 – back to queuing – things seemed to have settled down quite a bit.

JW: Things had changed, thankfully – but what about that advertising hoarding! In the 1950s, of course, for a

few pounds some top footballers would happily advertise cigarettes, even as a health supplement. Many still smoked in the sixties, including in the tunnel on the way out to the pitch. But the idea, approaching the millennium, that it was okay to depict a man protecting a giant pack of cigarettes over his own wife in front of young supporters like these seems outrageous now, and for all kinds of reasons. In the stands and on the terraces in the 1990s you could still be watching the game through a fug of smoke. Smoking at football was still expected rather than outlawed. Today we sell cigarettes like hard drugs, under the counter and expensive, in little brown parcels.

SRC: If we take a little of what kills us, in fact we might emerge stronger seems to be the philosophy here. After all, we all suffer for our clubs, through all four seasons and changeable weathers, and we can stumble about for decades through a trophy desert. Few clubs in football win anything much.

JW: It would be harsh, I think, to say that football sets out to make its fans suffer. Early clubs could not afford a roof to protect terrace fans, so supporters often had to cling together in rain and snow, simply to try to stay warm and dry.

But there was the view at that time that standing out, unprotected, in all weathers was somehow character-building, good for you. Even if you were busy passive smoking. Football supporting equals national service sliced up ninety-two times. Working men were hardy souls. Manual work was often dangerous and usually outdoors, and local football support was historically rooted in local working-class allegiances.

SRC: British football fandom has always been, at some level, about embracing suffering – proving your devotion, as you wait for the good times to come. By contrast, the USA's attempt at establishing 'soccer' never went down the smoking and suffering route: they just introduced popcorn instead.

'A Skinhead At Heart' - Ipswich Town, 2015

(SRC)

CHAPTER 7

The 'Derby' Between Us

SRC: In every pantomime, there must be a villain. Therefore, for every football club supported, there must be someone potentially to hate. Is that not true? In Britain, in media speak, we like to think of these as 'fierce' rivalries, but most British football derbies are actually quite mild.

JW: The term 'derby' for a local football rivalry in Britain probably comes from the ancient Ashbourne folk game, which is still played in *Derbyshire* today. We have our problems here; local rivalries can get out of control. But in some other countries fan rivalries can mean setting out to seriously damage or even kill each other, with flares, knives, and even guns being taken to the match.

Dundee and Dundee United in close proximity
(Courtesy of Google Maps 2018)

SRC: Raised in England on watching Watford FC – hardly Argentina's Boca Juniors, I concede – I was encouraged to seriously dislike, to hate in fact, our local rivals Luton Town. Away from my family and football friends and now in adulthood, I can actually admit today to having a bit of a *liking* for the Hatters of Luton. After all, they helped me

become the Watford supporter I am. But let's get some perspective here: the scale of the Watford versus Luton rivalry – and the geographical connections which brought these clubs together (down the main M1 motorway) – are nowhere near as powerful or as meaningful as the northeast Newcastle versus Sunderland standoffs, or the local derbies in Manchester, Sheffield, Merseyside, or Glasgow. Or even the one which still divides the city of Dundee in Scotland.

JW: Growing up, I remember seeing so many aerial photographs of the Dundee grounds in football annuals. The backstory was always: 'The closest football clubs in the world, less than 200 yards apart – both on the same street.' Only in Britain could two major sports stadiums grow up quite like this, bumping up against each other in the same neighborhood and in the same sport. The new football marketing men of today would almost certainly say: 'Rationalize your assets for pity's sake – share a stadium.'

SRC: Try telling British fans to share their home with a rival. They would tell you to get lost. Actually, that concept of sharing, which is intended as up-sizing, really does upset British fans even more perhaps than losing the local derby.

JW: There is little territorial divide for fans in Dundee, which means that people from both clubs live in each other's pockets or even share the same families. There is no escape in the 'big village' when your team loses the derby, but nor do people try to tear each other's heads off after the match.

SRC: Even today at Dundee, the visiting players in suits, carrying their boots, walk from their home dressing room

'Hands Across The Rivalry' - Sunderland v Newcastle United, 2007
(SRC)

up/down the road to their near-neighbors on derby match days. Some of the crowd join them. It's like a protest, but with nothing to protest about. It's fabulous that this can still happen.

Are the 'best' derbies the ones where two sets of fans are going as close as they can to hatred, without crossing a line? You often hear people say about rival fans, 'They absolutely hate each other,' but they say it almost with admiration. Less often do you hear them say: 'How nice: they all walk down the street together.'

JW: That friendliness is surely for middle-class rugby crowds. Without disrespecting the friendly Dundee stroll, a football derby has to have some intensity of feeling: resentment, envy, arrogance, mutual intolerance, call it what you like. But I would always stop short of hatred; this isn't war.

Just look at your picture of the famous north-east derby. Every fan from my generation who has ever traveled to an away fixture will probably have a story to tell about this kind of setup. The guy standing out in the Sunderland shirt seems to be in his own bubble, completely oblivious to the goading of the Newcastle lot. They just happen to live fourteen miles apart, brought up in different sporting tribes. So, by the rules of football fan engagement, they're actually from entirely different worlds, especially on derby day.

SRC: They have their separate tribal colors, these rivals, but at other times these fans probably go to some of the same bars, restaurants, and music gigs. But in the foreground, one can still see a sporting handshake across the barricades, a couple of older guys who probably feel like they've seen it all before.

JW: Football certainly does have that 'the enemy of my enemy is a friend' thing going on. The bitter Liverpool versus Manchester United regional derby only got really toxic in the 1980s, when Liverpool were doing most of the trophy winning, but Liverpool claimed United got too much of the media attention for its glamor and star players.

When United finally started dominating the English game in the 1990s, the Liverpool envy fizzed right down the connecting M62 motorway. Those United versus Liverpool fixtures became poisonous, but Liverpool got on fine with Manchester City and Leeds United fans. Why? They all found reason to despise United.

'England 2 Scotland 0' - M6 Motorway, 1996
(SRC)

SRC: The idea that you might hate your local Sheffield rival so much that you would even have their name tattooed right the way up your arm smacks more of love and respect to me. After all, you end up going to bed every night sleeping with the name of your bitterest enemy inscribed on your body – and it's forever.

'A Loving Arm' - Sheffield United at Sheffield Wednesday, 2012
(SRC)

In my chart of best derbies is one most people have never heard of: Auchinleck Talbot versus Cumnock Juniors in the West of Scotland, near where Bill Shankly was born. Okay, it's well below the radar of most people, but years ago, big Tom Wharton the giant of Scottish international refereeing heard I was off to photograph at Auchinleck. He grimaced and told me: 'You'd better take your steel umbrella, laddie; hatred shall rain down upon thee.' Biblical Big Tom knew what he was talking about because he had refereed plenty of spicy Celtic-Rangers derby games in his time. And he was indeed right. Before ninety minutes were up, there were rocks scattered all over the pitch from the humiliated Juniors' fans who were leaving the ground early, via the back alley.

JW: Football derbies in Britain can be a powerful stage for dramatizing political, ethnic, or faith differences, but its strongest rivalries are often simply about geography and localism. Burnley versus Blackburn Rovers, for example, has been a pretty intense local derby for around 140 years. All kinds of special arrangements are made to keep the peace. That pent-up East Lancashire macho pride has been nicely brewing and expressed around football. Some of these rival supporters can barely look at each other unsupervised.

SRC: Burnley actually advertises this fixture at Turf Moor as 'Burnley versus -------,' always leaving blank the opposition space because they know that the Burnley fans would just tear down any mention of Rovers.

There are also derby rivalries which bring together very different types of town. In Lincolnshire where I live

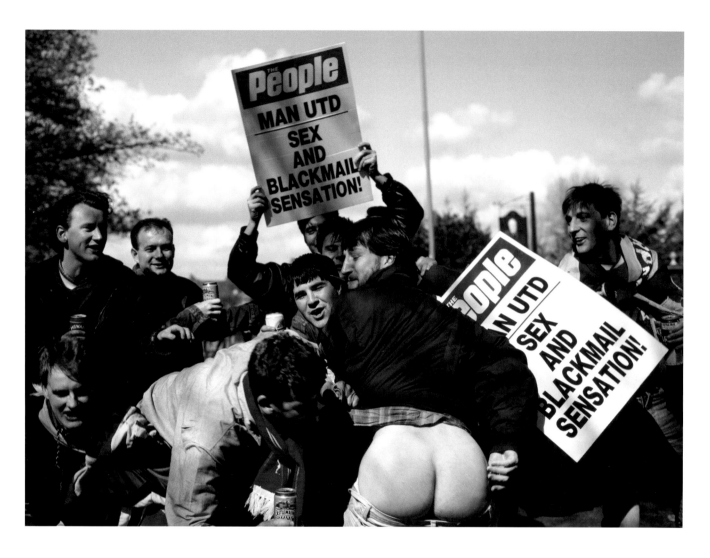

'Liverpool Fans Cruelly Expose Manchester United' - Aston Villa, 1990
(SRC)

now - a bit of a Bermuda triangle for football success - we've got Scunthorpe [United] known for its iron and steel, Grimsby [Town] for its fishing industry, and Lincoln [City], which lays claim to an airborne heritage - that lofty cathedral - but also via its surrounding RAF airfields. Memories of Lancaster Bombers and Spitfires. At home matches at Lincoln's Sincil Bank today, the old air-raid siren is still wound up and the crowd loves it. We know already about the 'football fishing fleet' from Grimsby, with boats named after football clubs of the day including, incidentally, Real Madrid. This gave local men a sense of pride in their vessel and a competitive edge to try to out-catch, say, a GY702 Huddersfield Town trawler.

JW: Sadly, British football also has its many unrequited derbies; those complicated local rivalries which can play out like the messiest of *ménage à trois*. In the East Midlands, for example, Leicester City fans like to eye up Nottingham Forest, European Cups and all. But Forest fans try to ignore Leicester - *their* rivalry is against Derby County. Westwards, just over the county line, Coventry City look on enviously. Can someone come and play with us? They dream of being Aston Villa's derby rivals, but the Villains couldn't care less: they have the Blues of Birmingham City in their own backyard to worry about. So each local meeting has its own juicy little subplot. Why can't you loathe us as much as we loathe you?

CHAPTER 8

Obeying The Laws

'Laying Down The Law' - **Burnley at Carlisle United, 1992**
(SRC)

'Stumbled Upon The Pitch' - **Carlisle United, 1992**
(SRC)

SRC: An amazing thing about British football is that you are just a few feet from multimillion-dollar players and multibillion-dollar match events and there is almost nothing to stop you striking out at a player, or running on the pitch and halting the game. But very few people do. In other countries they may need fences, moats, armed guards, and snarling dogs to keep the fans at bay. We want none of that now. Believe it or not, I think we have become quite trusting of each other at British football.

JW: There are the laws of the game, and there are the laws beyond it, which smack of social lore. Some instructions have become real laws, like not invading the pitch (1991 onwards), but most things governing fan behavior are unwritten laws - codes of conduct, really. Racist behavior and racist chanting was made an offense by law, in 1991. But to this day it's not wholly enforceable. Rather, it is down to the people - the fans - not to be racist or homophobic

and not to entertain hearing it from anyone else. It is hard to stop people having racist attitudes or to deal with individual instances of racism or homophobia inside the ground. But the anti-racist campaigns in Britain have been pretty successful. Problems seem much worse abroad. I think the way the game has globalized in Britain has also had a positive impact on fans. It's not easy shouting racist abuse when half the team you're supporting is recruited from around the world.

SRC: In Britain it's about trust, which goes hand in hand with freedom of speech. The police allow rival fans to be within shaking-hands distance because most people respect the need to keep the atmosphere going in a genuine way. Authentic is arguably what the British do well.

JW: But that trust does break down occasionally, usually

'High-Kicking Cantona' - **Manchester United at Maine Road, Manchester City, 1996**
(SRC)

because fans get angry and frustrated at owners or officials. But Hillsborough did teach us about the dangers of policing and stewarding and the fatal risks of fencing – a very expensive lesson. Problems among some fans in Europe and South America seem to be growing, with re-emerging forms of extreme nationalism and intolerance often expressed at football. We can't discount it returning to the UK.

SRC: These changes have attracted more black British fans, so our football grounds are beginning to feel much more like who we really are today. Do you remember

there used to be all that signage – quite comical actually – outside grounds, which gave a list of the things you weren't allowed to take in? Smoke canisters; guns; livestock, etc. But they didn't ever cover racist attitudes. Nor did they provide a picture prohibiting someone from violent swearing, like the signs you sometimes get in old public swimming pools.

JW: What about when players invade fans' spaces? Not in an Eric Cantona aggressive way, but when players throw themselves into the crowd in celebration. Surely, we want a bit more of that in our game: moments full of cathartic

An early pitch invader mocks the masculinity of the Everton goalkeeper Gordon West,
Liverpool v Everton at Anfield, September 1967
(Mirrorpix)

love between players and supporters. At times like these, when you get that mass celebratory hug on the touchline, it can seem as if the boundaries between players and fans really do dissolve a little. You can almost believe at such moments that footballers might even love the club as much as you do. At least, that is, until the next transfer window.

SRC: Referees often caution players for this sort of ecstatic abandon: *dangerous and against the laws of the game*. But it might be more against the spirit of football to be quite so harsh. Perhaps we should caution or send off

any referee who is so boring as to just go by the letter of the law and stop the fun.

JW: These incidents are different from the determined pitch invaders, the guys who are uncontrollably angry, perhaps at the board, the referee, or the manager. You can see why players and officials might be fearful about this kind of intrusion. Is he aimed at attacking me? Is he armed? Police or stewards chasing supporters onto the sacred turf can be a welcome and humorous distraction for fans. Will they catch him, or her? How many items of clothing can a fan successfully leave behind in the flailing hands of his pursuers? Will the invader get back into the crowd? Should we boo or cheer them?

SRC: For a while it became almost a requirement in this country that you had a sporting streaker: at football, rugby, and even at cricket. Are these 'soft' intruders treated differently from someone who invades the pitch with a bit more malice? I wouldn't be surprised if they eventually get let back into the ground, maybe wearing the groundsman's spare overcoat.

There can also be a serious 'political' breaking of rules at football, a bit like the mass trespass on Kinder Scout in 1932 in the Peak District to protest at walkers being denied access to areas of open country. Sometimes, there may be no other way to put across a point than to demonstrate on, and off, the pitch. Coventry City pitch invaders at the Ricoh Stadium in 2016 were aiming to get their hopeless hedge fund owners SISU out and even the local police seemed to be supporting them. Other Coventry fans had earlier refused even to go into the ground. The club chairman responded by saying that organized pickets like these were a case of *lions being led by donkeys*. Naturally, the fans then dressed up as both. When Coventry City were sent down the M1 motorway in the 2013/14 season to play 'home' games at Northampton Town, some City fans followed in their animal heads and gathered on a hill outside the stadium.

JW: Fancy dress at the season's end has become an invented tradition at British football grounds. Supporters find it a bit more difficult to lose their heads if they are dressed up. But officials don't like protests - breaking the rules - but demonstrating at football has definitely become more inventive, a lot more theatrical. And much more necessary.

SRC: Those protesting Coventry City supporters at Northampton look positively Shakespearean. But players and coaches can also be pulled up for supporting 'political' causes at matches. A goal-scorer can drag up his shirt to reveal a message that says he 'Loves Jesus,' but not one that says the same about striking workers. Manchester City manager Pep Guardiola's Catalonian yellow ribbon also upset England's Football Association.

JW: Subtly, or not, supporters invariably drape stuff over the perimeter hoarding, including themselves. Which

'Donkeys And Lions Together In Protest'
Coventry City at Northampton Town, 2014
(SRC)

pisses off the club's commercial director, sponsors, and club partners. Today's supporters are more likely, instead, to club together and hire a small plane to deliver their complaint or 'joke.' Meanwhile, owners and managers have become much more thin-skinned, more vulnerable in the media spotlight.

SRC: And to ram this home, there's Twitter: 'Sell our club to someone who wants to be here before it's too late.' Owners and managers wait for the next fan performance or intrusion, but rather than worry about this happening on or near the pitch, they are probably more worried today about social media; they can never quite be sure if the law protecting freedom of speech is about to deliver an uncomfortable rude-awakening 280-character post addressed to them. Even if they choose to ignore such *advice*, many, many others will see it.

JW: Who would be in charge of a football club in the internet age?

CHAPTER 9

A Game Of Modest Invention

SRC: The game is often said in casual conversation to have 'changed beyond all recognition.' But I don't think it has – not on the pitch at least. Its simplicity is still its charm. Instinctively, I think we know that the game is pretty much how we want it to be. If there are any changes to be made, they are usually made grudgingly, gradually, increment by increment.

1959 advert for the oldest sports brand in the world, relaunched as Mitre
(Mirrorpix)

JW: I would say that football adapted quickly right at the start. Initially, players could catch the ball – but not run with it – and the early game under FA laws still had mass pile-ups to try to force the ball forward. As the use of the hands for outfield players disappeared and football became more competitive and more professional, we needed neutral referees to deal with fouls and contentious decisions. Ex-private-school players were unhappy. They argued that no true gentlemen could commit fouls, so they abhorred the awarding of penalty kicks as an attack on their character. Upper-class footballers might miss

spot kicks on purpose, just to make a point.

We had the revised offside law in 1925, of course – which led to more goals and a new defensive position, the stopper center-half. But I suppose the role of the goalkeeper has changed most over time. Keepers get a bit more protection now compared to the days when they got kicked around and barged into the net. Goalkeepers could handle the ball (but not run with it) anywhere in their own half until 1912. Leigh Roose, a Welsh goalkeeper, liked to bounce the ball (and his opponents) outside his area and when he retired the law change was made.

Bournemouth and Boscombe's Jack Bradford, 1930
(Mirrorpix)

SRC: It took another eighty years, though, for football's leaders to decide that it was a bad idea to let keepers handle the ball if it was passed to them by defenders in trouble.

'The Inswinging Corner Kicker' - **Stockport County, 1990**
(SRC)

JW: Goalkeepers are a little less detached from their teammates these days, and the notion that if you couldn't play you got stuck in goal has long disappeared. Today's keepers need to be as smart with their feet as they are with their hands. Pep Guardiola's way at Manchester City is a new version of 'total football' where even the man between the goalposts is super-slick at passing the ball outside his own penalty area.

SRC: And what about heading? I think it's almost over for 'heading a ball.' Ex-players have started looking into this, fearing what may lay ahead. There are so many cases of ex-players having dementia. Balls of almost any fabric, except beach balls, when at speed are much like missiles to the head.

Incidentally, I myself often get hit on the back of the head when busy photographing the crowd with my back to the pitch.

JW: You do know that wingers were supposedly rated by old-school center-forwards by how well they could present a sodden leather football so that it could be headed cleanly, away from the ball's laces? Otherwise, it was a Saturday night out for the center-forward with an ugly facial lace imprint. If heading does go from the game – it's already banned for kids in the USA and Scotland – say goodbye, too, to the British corner and long-throw specialists. No more jumping around at the ball (and opponents) in the penalty box, so much a part of the British game.

SRC: When you think about it, the throw-in has always been a bit of an anomaly in football. You have this fantastic, high-skill game all about keeping the ball moving by preventing the use of the hands – sheer genius. But when the ball goes out of play on the sidelines you allow it to be picked up and *thrown* back in. Why? You take a corner *kick*, so why take a throw?

JW: The throw-in probably came from the sport in the private schools when handling and kicking were both still allowed. Taking a threatening corner kick today is not an easy skill. Coaches demand much more. Look at the number of corners that are floated in, over-hit, or don't even get past the first defender. At night, under lights, a corner can sometimes seem like a lonely delivery into the unknown. Where are your targets, your teammates? Is anybody out there?

BBC Radio Times coverage to help listeners follow the game, 1927
(Mirrorpix)

SRC: Fans elsewhere are always intrigued by the British response to being awarded a corner. We get really excited, our center-backs piling in with the forwards and then the usual argy-bargy starts in the box. Pure theater.

But on the continent, getting a corner is not quite such a big deal, just another means of restarting play. At Barcelona in Spain, they like taking corners short, as if it is rather vulgar to try to score by simply pumping the ball into the penalty area. Historically only 4 percent of Premier League corners result directly in goals. So why get so excited? We do, anyway.

JW: One major change in our thinking about football came when broadcasting came along. We did then have to 'reinvent' the game for people who were not in the stadium when the BBC started broadcasting matches live on the radio in 1927; they tried to make the game more meaningful for people at home by providing, in the *Radio Times*, a helpful grid guide to the pitch.

SRC: So, this was another modest adjustment, one helping to communicate the game to a wider public. Listeners checked out the grid whilst listening to the commentator. In the background, an assistant was navigating you around the field by shouting out square numbers.

JW: It sounds crazy, I know, but it's actually quite a clever idea, much ridiculed since. When you listen to football on the radio now, can you ever really work out what's going on, or exactly where the play is? I doubt it. The saying 'Back to square one' might have come from these first radio football commentaries. Sounds plausible to me. Listening to football on the radio allows for your imagination to do most of the work – and you can also feed the cat or wash the car at the same time.

SRC: Historically, preparing players was rarely very sophisticated in British football. We saw it as a straightforward game, combining perspiration with natural talent. Training to play meant being shouted at by ex-military men, rather like those infantrymen bounding out of the trenches. No need for complex coaching or tactical schooling.

JW: The British game is chock-full of stories of tannerball players with God-given talent and old-style club trainers who told their less gifted men: 'No need for work with the ball this week. You can get hungry for that at the weekend.' British football has always been seen as a bit of a battle, more brawn than brains, more desire than tactics.

Bill Shankly and his young Huddersfield Town players,
training on rough ground, May 1, 1959
(Mirrorpix)

Even the visionary Bill Shankly had his Huddersfield Town players training on a car park when times were hard. When he moved to Liverpool in 1959, Shanks had his young stars playing training matches against local garbage men.

SRC: Around the same time that Shankly was playing games in car parks, there was a great leap forward in the use of photographs to help tell the story of the match.

There is an action shot at Old Trafford in the early 1960s which feels to me like a very traditional English football scene on a typical winter's day in industrial Manchester. The floodlight pylon echoes the factory chimney, so the industrial roots of the game seem especially clear in this picture. It also shows the intensity and physicality that's still so important to the British – this goalkeeper is about to risk real injury here, possibly a boot in the face. We can also see in the foreground another photographer to the one taking the picture, doing his job, included as part of the event. This is quite an arty composition.

Sports photographers around the time of the *Bobby Charlton-about-to-boot-the-ball-and-goalie-into-the-net* real action shot started using telephoto lenses, which meant that they could appear to get closer to the action, whilst not actually being quite so close. You could now photograph goalmouth action from up the other end of the pitch – the goalie lying injured after a clash with Bobby Charlton, or an incident involving a skinhead in the crowd.

West Ham goalkeeper Standen dives at the feet of Bobby Charlton to prevent a goal-scoring opportunity. Manchester United, 0, v West Ham United, 1, October 1963
(Mirrorpix)

Photographers could now do all of this from far away, from a safe distance. And, of course, without having the faintest idea what was truly going on.

JW: Over time, fans' relationships with photographers and the media have changed in complex ways, whilst links between fans and players have become ever more distant. That intimacy of meeting for a beer after a game with a top player in the local bar has pretty much gone, certainly at the highest level. 'Text me,' says someone who may be stood only a few feet away. And yet social media can give the impression of a new kind of direct connection to the stars.

Twitter can offer an idea of what goes on behind the scenes, but it is a very managed picture. How can we get a look behind the curtain? In Manchester City's exclusive new Tunnel Club, corporate fans can now watch that sacred moment before the game when players are twitching and eyeing up the opposition in the players' tunnel.

SRC: For photographers, once color arrived in the 1960s the use of black-and-white film lent the subject a certain kind of artistic depth. One of reserve, of distance – of another time. Color is the stuff of cheap polaroids and family albums, something you owned yourself rather than something the photographer showed you. This is *Mad Men* territory of course. Newspapers typically told the story in black and white, shades which were beyond most people's emotions and experience.

JW: I guess you could say that in the last thirty years or so in England, we have seen an increasing 'coloring-in' of the game and a softening of its outline. Some might even say we've been 'feminizing' English football culture, making the sport progressively more accessible to others.

Elton John, superstar, leading Watford FC out
for training at Vicarage Road, April 1974
(Mirrorpix)

'The Singing Stand' - West Bromwich Albion, 1994
(SRC)

As top clubs have monetized the brand, that process has created a commercial energy but also a warmth inside stadiums, rather than chasing the more authentic, but sometimes hostile, conditions of the past. We are in that second generation of the 'family atmosphere' and greater inclusivity inside English football grounds – which is, itself, an invention.

SRC: I would say some of that began much earlier at Watford FC, the club I supported as a boy. The Vicarage Road stadium went from being a few blokes dotted about on crumbling terraces (I remember a guy in a string vest we called 'The Man with The Bag' pacing about yelling, and always threatening to leave) to becoming a club and a ground which was much more welcoming. It was a place that came with a certain Elton John attached. The chairman's aura - even when he was not physically there – somehow filled a void. He seemed to color the place gold and black, thus lifting drab little Watford. Parts of the stadium began to be named after sponsors but also after people who had made clubs into what they were. People like Watford's much loved coach Graham Taylor. For good or ill, labels such as East, West, South, North, Kop, and Enclosure would largely be confined to history as grounds were rebuilt.

JW: Your memories about Watford FC are a very useful reminder to me that if you look back through the 1960s and 1970s with too much nostalgia, you realize that lots of football grounds were at best functional and at worst pretty shabbily constructed. For every classic Archibald

Leitch design from the past or careful later additions to his themes, there were football grounds which had some individuality but were also architecturally pretty uninspiring.

SRC: In the post-Hillsborough redevelopment phase for British football stadiums, we now had a new color palette and computer technology was widely available to us. I would say that we did have some examples which reconnected good design with the necessary art of putting a roof over fans' heads.

An obvious example was the new stadium for

Sunderland framework all ready for the new stand being erected
at the Fulwell end of Roker Park, July 1964
(Mirrorpix)

Huddersfield Town. I was able to photograph throughout the building process, which saw Town's historic ground (where the club won its league titles back in the 1920s) make way in 1994 for a revolutionary new, banana-roofed structure. Fans could watch it grow. I remember the local excitement when this amazing stadium started to sprout up – and in what most people had dismissed as just a humble northern town that had seen better days.

Even when it was only half-completed, it won a national award for 1995's best new building. Not just the best new *sports* building, but the best new *building* of any kind. What a feather in the cap for the club and the game. When it opened, you had a real sense of being part of something truly inspirational for the neglected north.

JW: The 1990s were important because, although I think we built too many 'identikit' stadiums, new grounds with far too little imagination, style, or identity of their own, the period also demonstrated that designing a new football ground could be prestigious and a source of civic pride once more.

The great difference between Britain and the USA, of course, is that American cities are desperate to attract sporting franchises – and they are scarce on the ground. So, cities and businessmen in the US are always willing to raise the funds to build you a snazzy new sports ground if you care to relocate. In Britain, football clubs are pretty much tied to one place (Wimbledon FC excepted) and you are on your own. Raise the cash and take your chances on getting the crowds to come. There are no 'boosterism' handouts here.

'East Corner Fortune' - Glasgow Rangers, 1992
(SRC)

SRC: Invention - the shaping of the game - can come from unexpected places. In a tiny town, Nailsworth in the Cotswolds, the smallest ever to host English League football (Forest Green FC only got in the League in 2017), they are pursuing 'another way' (also the name of the street on which their current ground is situated). They are the first and only vegan football club in the world. Their green credentials go beyond their team wearing green and the club allowing no meat to be sold around the ground… they also have a solar-powered robot mowing every blade of their grass. It does so all the time and should it encounter an obstacle it sends a text message to the [human] groundsman and is programmed to go back to that same spot later. The club's second new ground

The new Forest Green FC stadium due to open in 2023
(Zaha Hadid)

'New Home On The Horizon' - Huddersfield Town, 1994
(SRC)

within twenty years will be an all-wooden stadium (shown in this chapter) built next to the M5 motorway.

JW: Will Forest Green ever get to share their greenness with the big boys, in the Premier League? Money and TV are driving the game, not greenness. Let's see how it evolves.

For now, mega-money satellite TV deals have brought football to millions in the UK and hundreds of millions more worldwide. Satellite TV's dynamic has challenged the power of the turnstiles and gate receipts as the main wealth-supplier for top clubs. Television had to get people to see the game its way – to crack the long-standing ritual of 3 p.m. Saturday kickoffs, for example – in favor of broadcast football every night of the week.

Who would ever have imagined that on a Monday night, at a time when most fans would be reflecting on what their team had done at the weekend, we would all be directed to watch yet *another* live game at home or in the pub? On one recent weekend in February 2018 the sports TV stations offered fans in Britain a reported twenty-three live matches from all over Europe. Will we keep on wanting to go to stadiums in the future as live football spreads on TV? I wonder.

CHAPTER 10

Final Score (Well, Almost)

'Holding Back Time' - Clydebank, 1995
(SRC)

JW: We are over halfway through our conversations. It feels right that we have a chapter at this point about the ritual of time itself, and its interruption. Times have changed, we say, as if we are heading towards something else. Something better? Something later? After halftime? A reckoning time?

SRC: What is it about halftime at a football match? The commentators often say about managers that they can 'hardly wait' to get their players in the dressing room, as if something magical can happen there. More importantly, it's as if halftime can actually stop time in its tracks. A chance to reset the clock, put things right.

JW: For the players and coaches, it is a chance to recalibrate. Where is it going wrong? What do we need to do to hold on? Managers can later use the halftime message to keep their own mystique alive. For fans, it's time for a leg-stretch and maybe a pee and a pie. For

broadcasters, an opportunity to dissect the match so far – and cram in the requisite adverts. One way the game has certainly changed at the top level is the computer-aided halftime expert analysis, but also the messing about with kickoff times. It was so much simpler when everyone kicked off at the same time, on the same day. In the days when all matches kicked off at 3 p.m. on Saturdays and finished around ten to five, sports newspaper men lived on their nerves. Most football grounds didn't even have a clock back then, so it was almost complete guesswork for fans (and editors) when games would end.

'Scoreboard's Winter Cheer' - Shrewsbury Town, 1991
(SRC)

SRC: At Clydebank, near Glasgow, there was something really novel: a guy whose role was no less than to 'hold back time' with a big stick until the referee started the game. Earlier, the same guy had been organizing the car park, directing traffic, a jack of all trades. Holding back time was just one of his many match-day jobs.

The Valiant Football League Ladders, 1965-66
(Valiant Annual)

JW: That is quite a talent. At halftime, before mobile phones intervened and when every match kicked off at three o'clock, there would also be roundups of all the scores around the grounds. The men inside their strange old ABCDEF huts [opposite] had one eye on the pitch and their ear to BBC radio. How quickly can we get the halftimes out? Or else you watched stewards walk slowly around the pitch carrying the score numbers to pin next to the halftime letters listed only in the match program. 'Is he carrying a five? Who can be five down at halftime?' 'Which match is D?' You could hear the crowd gasp as an outlier score went up: 'Shrewsbury beating Watford 4-1! At halftime!' The buzz would go around all the grounds.

SRC: Scoreboards really only grabbed you for a few minutes around halftime. Once you got tuned into the important national developments, the scoreboard attendants could get back to watching their own match, and with a grandstand view. I think this connecting up of all these local skirmishes to the national football battle was part of the enjoyment of everyone playing at the same time. Afterwards, the *Evening Pink* or *Football Green* newspapers were printed all around the country with match reports, results on the front page, and late scores. All this within thirty minutes of matches ending. How did they do it?

JW: My dad used to send me out to get the pink *Football Echo* on Saturday evenings in Liverpool. Queues of working men outside local newsagents and sweet shops.

If Everton had been at home they would get the front-page story, Liverpool the back. Blazing headlines were routinely in play: 'Reds/Blues see off Gunners/Hammers.' Our smaller regional neighbors, Tranmere Rovers, Southport, Wrexham, and Chester, would all have their own short match reports. A bit of rugby league – Liverpool City, St. Helens, and Wigan – was on the back page. You could tell what had happened in the big local games because there was always a little drawing of a Kopite [Liverpool] and a Toffee Lady [Everton] at the top of the front page. They would dance wildly if their team had won, be downcast in defeat, or hold a point on a flat hand for a draw. A little bit of cartoon magic for the kids.

'Reporters On Laptops And Urn Of Tea' - Sunderland, 1991
(SRC)

SRC: For those supporters not walking to the game, but who instead had legged it back to the car to tune into the radio, another match-day tradition awaited. Bang on 5 p.m. on Saturday – and it's still happening now, complete with the same piece of music that has accompanied it for generations – is the reading on the BBC of the Classified Football Results. (There was something very definitive about that word 'classified.') For forty years, the results were read by James Alexander Gordon, with his lovely Scottish brogue. Then (revolution here), a woman, Charlotte Green, was in charge on BBC radio, with an equally soothing, but authoritative, voice. Voice pitch *up* for a winning score, down for a defeat. Level it out for the spoils shared. Charlotte nailed it. Despite the Sky and BT alternatives, this ritual still tells us about places in Britain

that we have never visited or ever imagined.

How could we know anything about them if it wasn't for the national football scores, read out every Saturday at 5 p.m.? Every senior club's name is still in there, fed into and spewed out by the BBC teleprinter using what seemed at the time like amazing and puzzling technology.

Recently, just when you think the scores have finally ended at some exotic and mysterious location in Scotland, a Stenhousemuir, or a Stranraer, the Welsh Premier League scores pop up. Devolution times. There is that feeling, especially in winter, that the whole nation was wrapped up in the same itchy, but warming, woolly blanket – of football.

JW: Look, things have moved on and complainers about change usually also love all the additional live football on TV today. So, let's try to rein in some of this nostalgia, because that's what it is. But you definitely did feel part of something which was widely shared back then – a nation's Saturday heartbeat – something that was being replicated, in real time, all over the country. As kids, we messed about with those 'high-tech' card football table ladders, which were given away free in comics. I dare say all this is done much better online now. And people also knew, back then, that you had your weekends clearly laid out. Saturdays for football; Sundays free for family time: walk the car, wash the dog, sell the kids. No internet or mobiles meant that match reporters were vital for most people's basic football information – yet they worked to punitive deadlines and in pretty primitive conditions.

SRC: The photograph of these press men at Sunderland was taken in the early nineties, when we were on the very cusp of major change. They have early laptops, but not the internet. It was still called 'the wire' back then, a form of telegram service. It's a homely image – check the carpet – even though the match was in fact a big one, Sunderland versus Arsenal.

Today, of course, everyone is a reporter, fans tweeting out comments as the game goes on, later ringing in the phone-in shows, usually enraged. You can see every goal online and some supporters even run their own little TV stations. But before the 2000s, we all hung on the written words of that gallant small gang of football press journalists. They probably spoke their account of games down a telephone line to a secretary, who didn't necessarily dig football, but typed it all up anyway. Today, the press pack is able to send their pictures and words

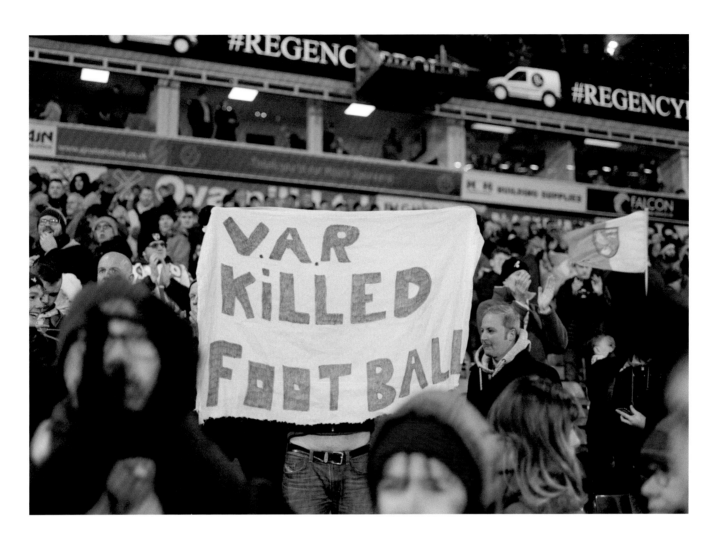

'The New Technology Is In Question' - Norwich City, New Year's Day, 2020
(SRC)

from a ground in a flash. We can also hear their views in seconds (if we really want to). And, whisper it, there are now even some *female* reporters.

JW: Spending time in the Premier League is what dictates exactly who wants to receive your message these days. How large is your prospective fan base today, how many supporters do you need to try to get your stories to? Information is money. And to some extent the clubs boss it: the British newspaper is no longer number one for club news. The clubs call the tune despite the fact that hundreds of thousands of people also want to (and do) weigh into the conversation. Some fan bloggers can have audiences reaching hundreds of thousands, and what the

TV pundits do or say is immediately part of the football story today, especially if they mess up somehow.

Top clubs churn out millions of PR stories and they and their sponsors try to control much more of what their players say. Journalists have to pick at what scraps of 'original' material they can get hold of. Everyone else has an opinion these days – and, apparently, we all have to listen to them. 'Experts' no longer hold sway and nobody tells us what has *really* happened on the field, not even VAR! We are all expected to make our own judgments – the game is 'all about opinions' as some idiotic pundits insist. It could be seen as a form of democratization, but I'm not sure we wouldn't be better back with those ABC halftime scoreboards.

Football's Timeline

OVER 200 MOMENTOUS YEARS IN BRITISH HISTORY

WITH

mitre®

1817 Benjamin Crook opens his tannery in Huddersfield, England, so the oldest sports brand in the world is founded - which later becomes MITRE

1845 The first written 'football' rules are produced by three pupils at Rugby School

1848 The Cambridge rules follow, with goal kicks, throw-ins, and forward passes

1857 Sheffield FC is formed, with claims to be the world's first football club

1862 Notts County FC is founded in the George Hotel in Nottingham, and are thus the oldest surviving professional football club in the world

1863 In London, meeting between ex-public-school men results in the world's first Football Association ('The FA') and some national laws for football

1866 Forward passing is accepted in the national laws

1871 A split in the FA ranks produces the Rugby Football Union for a game mainly played using the hands

1872 Wanderers FC beat Royal Engineers in the first FA Cup final, at the Kennington Oval. Scotland play England in a 0-0 draw in the world's first international fixture

1875 The introduction of a crossbar to replace tape between two poles is approved

1876 March 25: Wales plays its first international match, a 4-0 loss against Scotland in Partick, Glasgow

1878 Newton Heath Lancashire and Yorkshire Railway FC is established, later to become Manchester United. Everton FC are also formed and move to play at Anfield in 1884. A dispute among the club's directors in 1892 will lead to the formation of Liverpool FC - and the departure of Everton to nearby Goodison Park

1881 The Scot Andrew Watson becomes the world's first black football international player

1882 The four Home associations meet in Manchester in December to try to agree on an early uniform set of rules/laws for playing football across national borders

1883 March 31: Blackburn Olympic become the first northern working-class club to win the FA Cup. No ex-private-school club will triumph again

1884 The first FA Amateur Cup final is staged in response to the increasing domination of the sport by professional clubs. Old Carthusians beat Casuals 2-1 at the Athletic Ground, Richmond

1885 The FA is forced to legalize professionalism after complaints from southern clubs about northern professionals in the FA Cup

1886 The International Football Association Board (IFAB) is established and it now guards the new international laws of the game

1887 The IFAB approves two major law changes. The duration of the match shall be ninety minutes and games should be played by eleven players on each side

1888 William McGregor, an Aston Villa director, leads on the formation of the twelve-club Football League

1889 Preston North End becomes the first club to win the Football League/FA Cup double

1890 Stoke become the first Football League club to fail to get re-elected. They joined the Football Alliance, which they won and thus were re-elected to the Football League

1891 The goal net, referees, and penalty kicks (the 'kick of death') are all introduced into the game

1894 Nettie Honeyball persuades thirty young women to join the first British Ladies Football Club

1895 March 23: The first officially recorded women's match takes place, at Crouch End, London

1898 Automatic promotion and relegation for two clubs is introduced into the two-division Football League

1899 For the first time, the top two league clubs face off in a last-day title decider. Aston Villa humble Liverpool 5-0 in front of 41,000 fans

1901 Under FA strictures, the Football League introduces a maximum wage for players of £4 per week into its regulations. Tottenham Hotspur become the first and only non-league club to win the FA Cup after the formation of the Football League

1902 April 5: The first major stadium disaster in British football, at Ibrox Park, Glasgow, kills 25 spectators

1903 The PFA is convened in Manchester originally as the Association of Football Players' and Trainers' Union

1904 The Fédération Internationale de Football Association (FIFA) is founded in Paris

1905 June 6: England's first international match against foreign opposition, a 6-1 victory in Austria

1909 Goalkeepers must now wear a shirt (a jersey) that is distinguishable from all the other players and the match officials

1911 Founded only in 1903 and immediately elected into the Football League Second Division, Bradford City win the FA Cup, still the club's only major honor

1912 The laws prohibit goalkeepers from handling the ball outside the penalty area; previously, they could handle the ball anywhere in their own half

1914 The King attends the FA Cup final for the first time. As war breaks out in August, the Football League decides to play on, to official consternation

1915 January 1: A letter written by a doctor attached to the Rifle Brigade is published in *The Times*, reporting on a football match played by British and German troops between the trenches in France. April 2: A Football League match between Liverpool and Manchester United is fixed by players on both sides

1917 The Dick and Kerr Ladies FC is formed in Preston, the most important of the early women's clubs

1919 As football reboots, the First Division is expanded from twenty to twenty-two clubs.

1920 Leading clubs from the Southern League join the Football League to form a new Third Division

1921 The wartime popularity of women's football leads the FA to ban women's clubs at its members' grounds

1922 A major expansion of the Football League to eighty-six clubs, with twenty teams added from the Midlands and northern England, means a truly national league

1923 April 28: The first Wembley FA Cup final sees chaotic scenes as the pitch is overrun by fans

1924 Herbert Chapman wins the First Division title for the first time, as manager of Huddersfield Town. The Town would go on to win three titles in a row, the first club to do so

1925 The offside law is changed from three to two players, thus producing more goals

1927 April 23: Cardiff City are the first and only non-English club to win the FA Cup, beating Arsenal 1-0. Another Welsh outfit, Aberdare Athletic, fail to get re-elected into the Football League, being replaced by Torquay United

1928 Everton's Dixie Dean becomes the first player to score sixty top-flight league goals in one season. No one since has matched the feat

1930 April 21: Leicester City and Arsenal draw 6-6, still the highest scoring draw at the top level in England

1933 April 29: The FA Cup final sees numbered shirts for players for the first time

1934 Goalkeeper Steve Milton of Halifax Town sets an English league record by conceding thirteen goals on his league debut, against Stockport County

1935 December 4: England host Germany at White Hart Lane, despite public protests about Hitler's policies

1936 Sunderland win the First Division title for a then-record sixth time. They remain the last club to win the league crown wearing striped jerseys

1937 A remarkable 147,365 fans watch the Scottish Cup Final, still a European record for a club match

1938 Stanley Rous, Secretary of the FA, rewrites and modernizes the laws of the game down to seventeen

1939 After making a speech at a match on Easter Saturday asking spectators to join up, club captain Harry Goslin and the entire Bolton Wanderers first team join the 53rd Field Regiment, Royal Artillery

1940 Tom Cooper of Liverpool FC, fifteen England caps, is the only England international player killed in the war. By April, according to *Picture Post*, 629 professional footballers had joined the services

1941 Playing and watching regional football, including clubs using guest players, remains hugely popular on the home front. After the end of the Blitz in 1941, match attendances rise steadily

1942 Many of England's top clubs are depleted – Liverpool saw seventy-six players sign up and Wolves ninety-one. The 1942 London Cup is won by Brentford FC. The competition only lasted two seasons, so the Bees remain the holders

1943 As in the First World War, women's factory teams are formed to play charity matches and aid with the war effort. Among them are aircraft factory teams, such as Fairey Aviation Company

1946 March 9: Some thirty-three spectators are killed at Burnden Park due to poor facilities and overcrowding

1947 Severe winter weather decimates fixtures, leading to postponements and the league's longest-ever season

1948 Ex-prisoner of war Bernhard 'Bert' Trautmann signs for St. Helens Town. Overcoming local anger, he would later play professionally for Manchester City, suffering a broken neck in a winning FA Cup final and being voted 1956 Footballer of the Year

1949 Portsmouth FC are league champions, the only southern club outside London to win the title

1950 England and Scotland play in their first World Cup finals, with England sensationally losing 1-0 to the United States

1952 After title disappointments in the previous five seasons, Manchester United finally end a 41-year wait for the First Division title, finishing four points ahead of rivals Tottenham Hotspur and Arsenal

1953 November 25, in the 'Match of the Century,' England loses its first fixture at Wembley, 6-3 to incomparable Hungary. Stanley Matthews finally wins an FA Cup winner's medal as Blackpool defeat Bolton Wanderers, 4-3

1954 May 23: A confident England seek revenge in Budapest – and this time lose by a record 7-1 score

1956 Chelsea win the league title for the first time, but are refused permission by the Football League to compete in the new European Cup competition

1956 Manchester United, under Matt Busby, ignore the Football League and become the first British club to play in the European Cup

1958 February 6: Manchester United's plane crashes at Munich airport, killing twenty-three, including eight players

1959 Bill Shankly joins Liverpool FC, from Huddersfield Town, as manager; an epoch begins

1960 The new Football League Cup is launched: Aston Villa defeat Rotherham United 3-2 in a two-legged final

1961 The £20 maximum wage cap is lifted. Johnny Haynes becomes England's first £100-a-week footballer

1962 December 26: Brian Clough retires through injury to become one of England's greatest-ever club managers

1963 May 15: Tottenham Hotspur win Britain's first European trophy, the European Cup Winners Cup, defeating Atletico Madrid 5-1 in Rotterdam

1964 The BBC TV football highlights show *Match of the Day* is launched. It continues to thrill and inform today. Three Sheffield Wednesday players are convicted of match fixing

1965 August 21: Keith Peacock of Charlton Athletic becomes the first substitute used in the Football League

1966 July 30: England win the World Cup at Wembley by defeating West Germany 4-2, after extra time

1967 May 25: Glasgow Celtic are the first British club to win the European Cup, defeating Inter Milan 2-1 in Lisbon. No other Scottish club would match this feat

1968 May 29: Manchester United win the European Cup, the first champions from England and just ten years after the tragedy of Munich

1969 The Women's Football Association (WFA) is formed and forty-four clubs attend its inaugural meeting

1970 February 7: George Best scores a record six FA Cup goals for Manchester United v Northampton Town

1971 January 2: The Ibrox Stadium disaster - a horrific sixty-six fatalities, people crushed on a stairwell at a Rangers versus Celtic match - completely overshadows Southampton winning the first Mitre Women's FA Cup

1972 November 18: The first official UK women's full international match sees Scotland 2, England 3, at Greenock

1973 October 17: For the first time, England fail to qualify for the World Cup finals, losing 1-0 to Poland

1974 Tottenham Hotspur receive a two-home-game ban from UEFA after the club's fans riot in Holland

1975 The Anglo-Scottish Cup is launched to replace the unloved Texaco Cup

1976 Future England boss, the thirty-two-year-old Graham Taylor, achieves the first success of his managerial career by winning the Fourth Division title with Lincoln City. He surprises all by taking over at Elton John's Watford, still in the Fourth Division - but they will soon be on the rise

1977 May 25: Liverpool win the European Cup in Rome, sparking a period of English successes in Europe

1978 Aberdeen FC boast Britain's first all-seated football stadium, at Pittodrie. November 29: Viv Anderson, the twenty-two-year-old Nottingham Forest defender, becomes England's first black full international player when he appears in the 1-0 friendly win over Czechoslovakia at Wembley

1979 May 30: Nottingham Forest's remarkable run under Brian Clough continues when they beat Malmö of Sweden 1-0 in the European Cup final, record signing Trevor Francis scoring the only goal

1980 March 1: Everton lose 2-1 at home to Liverpool in the Merseyside derby, and during the game legendary former striker Dixie Dean dies from a heart attack in the stands, aged seventy-two

1981 Three points for a win is introduced, and QPR becomes the first club in Britain to install an artificial pitch

1982 An expanded FIFA World Cup finals kicks off in Spain with a record twenty-four countries competing. Italy triumph

1983 Tottenham Hotspur form a holding company to evade FA restrictions on profits and directors' salaries

1984 Liverpool FC win a historic treble of trophies: the league title, the League Cup, and the European Cup

1985 The Bradford fire and the Heysel Stadium disaster in Brussels signals British football's darkest year yet. League attendances the following season will slump to a postwar low of 16.5 million

1986 Alex Ferguson joins Manchester United as manager: thirty-eight trophies follow in twenty-six years at Old Trafford

1987 Burnley FC stave off a final day relegation from the Football League, thus extending their ninety-nine years of membership - and promising a later return to the top flight

1988 Scunthorpe United build the first new purpose-built Football League stadium in England for thirty-three years

1989 April 15: The Hillsborough disaster means the deaths of ninety-six Liverpool fans at an FA Cup semifinal. Mo Johnston becomes the first Catholic to sign for Glasgow Rangers in the club's 107-year history. He had already played for Celtic, 1984-87

1990 Liverpool's long domestic dominance is over, as heavy underdogs Crystal Palace defeat the Reds in a turbulent FA Cup semifinal at Villa Park

1991 The FA publishes its *Blueprint for Football* sanctioning, in 1992, a breakaway FA Premier League

1992 The FA Premier League is founded on the back of satellite TV money. The UEFA Champions League is also launched to replace the old knockout European Cup competition

1993 **Manchester United become the first Premier League champions while ending a twenty-six-year title wait.**

1994 The first FIFA World Cup finals held in the USA are deemed a great success, contributing to the launch of Major League Soccer two years later. Huddersfield Town move from run-down Leeds Road to the impressive new Alfred McAlpine Stadium at Kirklees, an early symbol of the regeneration of the English game

1995 **The Bosman ruling allows players in the EU to move at the end of a contract without a transfer fee**

1996 Arsène Wenger arrives at Arsenal, to manage 1,235 games over twenty-two years - and transform the English game. December 22: Peter Shilton, at Leyton Orient FC, becomes the first footballer to make 1,000 league appearances in English football

1997 **A unique season for Middlesbrough FC. Runners-up in both domestic cup finals, they are relegated from the top level after player illness means they fail to fulfil a league fixture against Blackburn Rovers**

1998 The Scottish Premier League is founded, breaking away from the Scottish Football League

1999 **December 26: Chelsea FC fields the first starting XI in top-level English football to contain no British players. May 8: Carlisle United goalkeeper Jimmy Glass makes history by scoring the 95th-minute goal that keeps his club in the Football League**

2000 The FA Cup final will not involve the holders, Manchester United, who withdraw from the 1999–2000 competition to play in the FIFA Club World Championship in South America, thus becoming the first FA Cup winners not to defend their title

2001 **Alex Ferguson, at Manchester United, becomes the first manager ever to win three successive English league titles**

2002 The collapse of debt-ridden ITV Digital in May plunges Football League clubs into crisis. Bradford City, Nottingham Forest, Watford, Barnsley, Lincoln City, and Port Vale all file for administration, fearful that the drastic revenue loss might put them out of business

2003 **Wimbledon FC relocates to Milton Keynes after controversially receiving permission to do so from the FA**

2004 Arsenal are the first elite English club since 1889 to complete an entire league campaign unbeaten

2005 **FC United of Manchester are formed by fans to protest the ownership of MUFC by the Glazer family from the USA. May 25: Liverpool FC stage the most dramatic European comeback in history to draw 3-3 with A.C. Milan in the Champions League before winning the trophy on penalties**

2006 Reading FC are promoted to the top flight for the first time in their history, after topping the Championship with a record 106 points

2007 **More Americans, Tom Hicks and George Gillett, buy Liverpool FC, bringing debt and later fan protests before the courts finally remove the owners in 2010**

2008 For the first time, two English clubs fight out the Champion's League final, as Manchester United beat Chelsea on penalties. Manchester City are taken over by the Abu Dhabi United Group, transforming them into one of the world's wealthiest football clubs

2009 **March 28: Frank Lampard scores the 500th England goal at Wembley in a 4-0 win over Slovakia**

2010 Portsmouth FC go into administration, the first Premier League club to do so, guaranteeing their relegation

2011 **Sky Sports TV's flagship presenters, Richard Keys and Andy Gray, are sacked for making crude, sexist remarks off air in the Sky studio**

2012 May 13: In a match thought to be the most dramatic ever, newly monied Manchester City score two stoppage time goals against QPR – the winner by Agüero - to snatch its first league title since 1968

2013 **Alex Ferguson, the most successful manager in the modern era, retires after winning his thirteenth Premier League title, all with Manchester United**

2014 England women's international player Fara Williams, once homeless, becomes the most capped player (140) in the history of English football

2015 **England women finish third in the World Cup finals in Canada, their best-ever performance**

2016 Leicester City, at initial odds of 5000-1, win the Premier League title

2017 **Lewes FC becomes the first club in Britain to pay its women's team the same as its men's**

2018 England reaches the semifinals of the FIFA World Cup in Russia

2019 **July 7: The USA wins the FIFA Women's World Cup in France and forward Megan Rapinoe becomes a global icon for her outspoken views on football, gender, and politics. October 14: England's players lead the way by threatening to leave the field after being racially abused by sections of the home crowd in Sofia, Bulgaria. There are Nazi salutes in the stands, signaling a disturbing trend in ethnic nationalism and fan behavior in many parts of Europe**

2020 Manchester City are banned by UEFA for two years from the Champions League for allegedly breaking Financial Fair Play (FFP) regulations. Matches all over the world are postponed or played behind closed doors as COVID-19 becomes a pandemic. Professional football is suspended in England, Scotland, Wales, and Northern Ireland from Friday, March 13. Suddenly Notts County, playing in the English fifth division, find they have the biggest gathering in the entire UK

CHAPTER 11

Playing 'Away' Is For Superfans

SRC: By my way of thinking, the game is best preserved today through sacrifice and through conversation. You get a lot of both when it comes to serious away travelers. Only 204 fans might make the 170-mile November trip, say, from Carlisle United in the far north of England to Grimsby Town, and they may not be specially feted by anyone for having done so (no one made them do it). But it is their noisy presence that is so invaluable for the integrity and survival of the game. The away contingent at smaller grounds is usually acknowledged by their hosts: the stadium announcer declares that 204 have made it, and thanks them for coming such a distance in such weather (he or she never accuses the opposition of a pathetic turnout, even if it is one).

JW: The Premier League has just started to cap away-match ticket prices at £30. It's a cheap win and a clear recognition that away supporters provoke the core atmosphere at most matches. Their singing and gentle (and not-so-gentle) abuse keeps the home fans on their toes and buzzing. And it is the away end you hear loudest on TV when a 'great atmosphere' is being discussed.

SRC: The British atmosphere is what foreign broadcasters often talk about when they take the Premier League feed. It's part of what they pay for. They like the spontaneous, boisterous fan rivalries we have here as part of the TV package, something which money can't really buy elsewhere. In Italy and Spain you might get more fan choreography – mosaics and rehearsed performances – but here we like something a little more organic. For us, supporters are not the main show, but they can add plenty to the pleasures of being there.

JW: We know that some supporters value only traveling away these days. They have given up on home support

Two policemen, helmets dislodged, try to control crowd disorder at the Spurs v Chelsea derby, White Hart Lane, April 1975
(Mirrorpix)

because it feels so passive, so uninvolving. Watching away means standing up, really supporting and calling your club home in hostile territory. It can feel more like the old days, more confrontational. The best songs are also usually invented away and players notice you, sharing victories but also commiserations in defeat. Winning together in a 'difficult' place feels much sweeter than any home win. You also recognize people later, fellow supporters who you might have met in the most inaccessible and risky places with your club. I saw Liverpool play in St. Petersburg against Zenit one icy and inhospitable February night, along with about 400 freezing Liverpool Reds. All are devoted heroes in my book.

SRC: I love the crisscrossing of football supporter travel routes that goes on in Britain, particularly on winter Saturdays. The service stations can be crazy places, as fans from all levels, traveling in all directions, briefly mix it up. 'Where are you going? We played there last week. Try the pies but look out for the stewards.' Mad places, too,

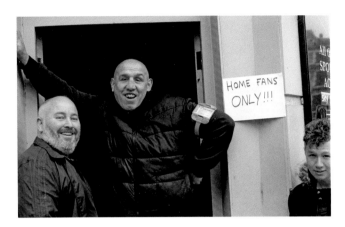

'Millwall Are In Town' - Wolverhampton, 2015
(SRC)

are some key railway stations, like Crewe near Manchester, truly a junction that almost every away football fan must have traveled through, or changed at, for an away trip at some point. Arriving at a destination railway station can be a challenge in itself: Where now? Follow the floodlights, follow the fans. For the FA Cup there might be a whole Dunkirk-like fleet of away-day match specials, tens of smart coaches followed by decrepit minibuses or weathered vans, usually filled with young guys whose drinking is monitored by older more experienced away travelers. Down the road they will be pulling up on a grass verge anyway, for a mass pee – or worse.

JW: Of course, some away fans will have to travel very much farther than others, especially those in the far north, or the English southwest, or from South Wales. A BBC survey in 2018 showed that an especially dedicated Plymouth Argyle fan had traveled around 12,000 miles in a single season to follow their club. Some supporters face traveling hundreds of miles just for home matches, regular 4 a.m. starts. Their local away fixtures might feel more inviting than the home ones. These are the sacrifices we make for football. But we might have it rather easy in Britain. After all, we are a relatively small nation with fairly decent transport routes. Consider this case: in March 2017, in the Russian Second Division, Luch-Energiya traveled to Baltika Kaliningrad for a league game. It was a single round trip made up of a cool 12,882 miles. I'm not sure how many away fans traveled, or if they felt the trip was really worth it – the match ended up a dire 0-0 draw. But we are back to the pleasures of suffering for football again, aren't we? I can still imagine a tiny band

of Luch-Energiya fans exalting later over a beer about the 'terrible' nature of the trip, but the rewards of actually being there when what might prove to be a precious point was brought safely back home. Could it have been done without us? I don't think so.

SRC: Countries on the scale of USA, Russia, or China tend not to encourage much away support. And even in Britain not all away fans are especially welcomed, though we're in the supposed post-hooligan era. Pretty much gone now are the days when large gangs of baggy-trousered, long-haired, and booted-up young 'lads' would parade up and down an unfamiliar high street, apparently looking for trouble. This show of visiting force – a gang mentality – wasn't always violent or lawless. But it looked impressive and its scale was often frightening to the afternoon shoppers. It also meant lots of running around and some welcome police overtime.

JW: The bark was often much worse than the bite. After Hillsborough, demand for away tickets began to change at the top level in England; different types of fans started to travel, women, lots more older supporters, and mainly season-ticket holders. But because of the forbidding reputation of some committed traveling fans, bars and pubs in distant places are not always that happy to see you arrive, even when you promise to behave yourself and drink the place dry.

'A Couple Enjoy A Lockout' - FC United at Colwyn Bay, 2011
(SRC)

'Arriving On His Horse Prop' - Mexico at Germany World Cup, 2006
(SRC)

'Collective Responsibility' - England v France at Lisbon, 2004
(SRC)

The city center can be pretty segregated now, as well as the stadium. But regular away fans who travel in small groups in cars can also devise their own checklist of 'quiet' bars on the away schedule. There is far more contented mixing of rival football fans before matches these days than some people who don't know the game might imagine or admit.

SRC: For me, a lot of the attraction of traveling away can still be about family bonding, sometimes with your dad, your brother, and even your grandad. And plenty more women watch away games these days; as you say it's a more civilized experience in the away end. Maybe this is because we intrepid football travelers are treated less suspiciously in the ground now, less like dangerous, marauding prison escapees and a little more like customers whose money is as good as anyone else's and whose safety is paramount. A side effect of this new friendliness is the mild disease of face-painting. It's part *Braveheart* and part creche at the local fete.

JW: I've wondered what you do if you are fully painted up but your team capitulates without a fight. Where do you go then? How long does the shame have to persist? Do you find a washroom right away, or just tough it out?

SRC: Fans of very small clubs don't bother with face painting. They have long enjoyed the gentler pleasures of away-match travel, when you can be on first-name terms with nearly everyone who goes. But the arrival on the non-

league scene of FC United of Manchester in 2005 shook up some of that low-key attitude to visiting supporters.

JW: Some clubs cashed in and began to charge extortionate admission prices for these games. Others complained about the rowdy behavior of some FCUM followers and wanted the club thrown out of the league. When the club joined the lowly North West Counties League Division Two, their opponents normally played before crowds of around fifty fans in total. FCUM produced an average of 1,200 away supporters (and a dog), a real challenge and a complete change of climate.

SRC: How did FCUM fans solve the excess away support issue? Find a friendly hill, turn each occasion into a party, and hob-knob with 'the enemy,' singing your hearts out, win, lose, or draw. It seems to work.

JW: What happens if you move in the opposite direction, to away support for national teams? Most people seem pretty comfortable in their own skins when they watch their country abroad. But a curious thing seems to happen at international level for the English. They don't entirely ditch their club identities – they bring them along for the ride. We get this complex merging of the national (the Cross of St. George) with the local (names of clubs, places, and friends on the flags) in a giant expression of a fragmented, but united, national/local solidarity.

The English have somehow become THE super away fans on the world stage.

CHAPTER 12

Saturday Afternoon, Sunday Morning

'Kirkbride The Captain Plays On' - Coniston, England, 1996
(SRC)

SRC: I wanted to try to say something through my photographs about village life, about the countryside and local football. This might sound quite straightforward, but it is actually surprisingly tricky. There's so much eulogizing about the countryside today, it's as if the city is to blame for all life's ills. There is also a spate of nostalgia about the supposed authenticity of the grassroots game – as though professionalism in football threatened to kill the goose that laid the golden egg in a once-leafier England all those years ago. We need to get over this.

JW: Grassroots football, especially outside big cities, for many people has come to signify something that is not yet spoiled, not gentrified. It is seen as green and pure, and with flourishing roots. In fact, some sports purists who may like football actually say that they prefer watching and playing the older game of cricket because they think cricket best reflects the gentle, pastoral elements

of English village life. It is played by locals, often neatly surrounded by a polite ring of supporters and volunteers, with (usually) female helpers making teas and scones. The vicar is probably next in the order to bat. This is John Major's vision of a bucolic England: the squire, cricket, and warm beer. Football has a job competing with that.

SRC: English cricket, when you come across it after turning some corner into a village, *is* like a rather beautiful vision of England in white flannels. It even has its own soundtrack: the rarefied, hollowed out, slightly delayed cracking sound of leather ball on willow. Some polite applause, birds tweeting. Cricket works a bit like the National Trust - like farmers preserving dry-stone walls - not so much to keep anything in or anyone out, but because it looks good to tourists and nostalgists.

JW: I think football works a bit differently in the countryside in that its role is partly to preserve the name and the standing of the village or small town; to keep together a group of lads (traditionally), a band of blood brothers, a cohort of young men almost awaiting a higher service. Which turned out to be the 'Greater Game' of war in the twentieth century. Local football teams - like war memorials - carry forth the names of places. They represent working men's identities in a way in which cricket, because of its perceived snobbishness, can sometimes find rather more difficult to do.

SRC: I have a village football tale to tell. I had recently arrived in the English Lake District (where as it turned out I was to spend the next twenty-eight years). I didn't have a local team and I thought a way to ingratiate myself with the local community was to roll up at the local club. Esthwaite Vale were not very good and had even folded and re-formed, but Coniston FC, they were legendary. So,

63

'Versus Lunesdale Afore Skiddaw' - **Braithwaite, the Lake District, 1994**
(SRC)

over the fell I ran with the farmer's pet dog who never got any exercise (I was lodging with his owners) and arrived in the pouring rain at the rickety bridge over a torrent of a stream beneath. Locals call this sort of heavy rain 'drizzle' and the water course a 'beck.'

Squinting through the rain splattering on the tin of the old changing room, I could just about hear a few voices inside. So I knocked on the door and it fell silent within. Then suddenly the door flew open and the players were all sat sideways, or standing, stretching in various states of undress. The senior player nearest the door yelled at me: *'AND WHAT THE F*** DO YOU WANT?,'* then slammed the

door shut. The soaking, shivering little dog looked up at me.

The door then opened slowly and they called me in. I got to train. To play. To be part of it. I swotted up on that legend of how, as a tough mining community (with a soft and gentle heart, of course) Coniston FC was certainly a club worth playing for. Fridays, spilling out of the Old Man (the mountain which gave everyone their living), the tin miners would race down the steep descent with their noisy steel-capped clogs, and into the village hall to find out if they were on Saturday's team sheet.

Carel Weight painting, 'Village Cup Tie,' 1946
(Courtesy of the owners, the Professional Footballers' Association)

JW: It's no surprise that the emblems and badges of so many professional clubs carry reminders today of their roots in lost local industries: the Blades, the Hammers, the Mariners (Sheffield United, West Ham United, Grimsby Town respectively). The connection between football clubs and local industries was pretty central right from the start.

SRC: For those selected for the Coniston team, who had already that day put in a hell of a shift down the mines, they could sit back and conserve their energy. Their next shift would be THE GAME. The squad players, however, could afford a drink or two and dance the evening away, promenading the local lasses into the night. Such was the close-knit nature of the community here, there were times when the entire first eleven was made up of just a few named families, the Walkers, the Kirkbrides, etc. To try to become more a part of this setup, on more than one occasion I actually slept in the old main stand – I felt I had years and years of catching up to do.

JW: It can grab you like that, the appeal of the football club as a route into the heart of the local [male] community. Scots who had moved to northeast towns and cities in England in the late nineteenth century often became members or shareholders in local football clubs to try to gain a foothold in urban civic life. It was the one way they felt they could demonstrate that they really belonged.

SRC: The photograph at Braithwaite [page 64] I took recounting my time in the Lake District league was even used as backdrop by Morrissey of The Smiths to one of his shows in Los Angeles. He was idealizing the kind of rural English masculinity I myself had found so engaging at Coniston.

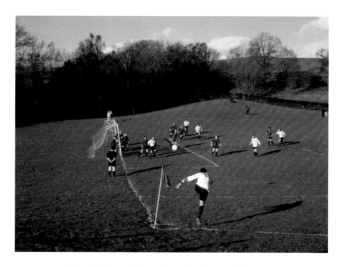

'Downhill From A Corner' - Heathwaite, Cumbria, 1997
(SRC)

to the neighborhood and village level and silhouetted against those beautiful, rolling Cumbrian hills.

SRC: My photographs of rural football, always without crowds, stands, or the spray-painted ultra-green pitches of the professional game, tend to look a bit bleak because they are so earthy and simple. I wanted to capture in this particular photograph where the game came from. This is deepest, rural Cumbria, but it's also the story of the very history of the game in Britain. These guys really are like the dry-stone wallers of sport. They are playing to keep their villages alive, but also to preserve that vision of the English countryside we all expect to see.

JW: So it is rather like those idealized images of rural and town sports one can find in a few famous paintings. The artist L.S. Lowry, of course, rather brilliantly captured the historic relationship between working communities and football in northern English towns, those deep connections between industry, working-class people, and the game.

One of Lowry's sports paintings, *The Football Match*, sold for £5.6 million in 2011, a record for one of his paintings. It's probably a year's salary for even a moderate Premier League player today.

'Continuing After The Match' - Edale, 2014
(SRC)

JW: I can see why Morrissey might go for it. He has a weakness for that kind of cultural juxtaposition. What I really like about this photograph – and I suspect Morrissey did too - is its essential informality and Englishness. In this country we play local football right down to the lowest level of organization. If you have a set of shirts you can hire a pitch, register your club, and play in a league. You need nothing else. These guys represent the very foundation of the English game, its roots deep down

SRC: The Carel Weight painting [previous page] on village football was completed just before *The Football Match*, so it comes from about the same period. It's from the collection owned by the Professional Footballers'

Association, based in Manchester. It has all the life and elements of the grassroots game, but we never see these elements on view in real life all at once, as you can do in a painting.

You can see here a serviceman edging onto the pitch. Perhaps he is returning from the war, or else waiting to be called up/selected? One of the women of the town is especially animated: dashing, poised, sprung, present. The goalie, in blood red, is punching the ball away, out of the frame and into the ether. Windswept trees and a dramatic sky suggest seasons passing and a real sense of urgency. A church is bang in the middle of the painting, along with the game at the very heart of village life. A painting does not tell 'the truth,' as we imagine a photograph does, but it can bring the defining elements of local life together, all in one scene.

'Hope Valley League Ref' - Stoney Middleton, 2014
(SRC)

JW: The reality in local football is that it is the collective that has to do everything to stage matches, something which is very important, I think. It is also a reminder that, not so long ago, young players had their own jobs to do inside professional clubs as part of their apprenticeships. They learned their trade by cleaning the boots of the senior pros, sweeping the terraces or painting the club stadium in the close season. There are fears today that some young elite players earn too much, have a sense of entitlement, and have it all too easy. Too much, too young.

SRC: Most of my grassroots photographs have a focus on space, and I try to keep them very simple. People's roles in staging games are also made very clear. The players I encountered do have to pull their weight, or there's no game. They have to do things for the club in the 'hands-on' sort of way that younger professionals or Academy lads no longer have to do.

The people in this vision of mine of local football are often shown working and muddied, obviously fully engaged. At Hathersage, I photographed (shown overleaf) a player in semidarkness - the changing room bulb had blown - having a shave ahead of playing in a match where very few people would be looking at him.

JW: Referees tend to be the forgotten men of the local game. They have no team to rally round and are often abused and left unconsidered. But without them local matches simply can't take place. Retired players can stay involved in the game by taking up the whistle, but it can

be a tough gig. In 2017 Ryan Hampson, an eighteen-year-old local league referee from Manchester, called a reported 2,000 local referees out on strike because of the way officials were being treated by both players and spectators.

SRC: Playing for a local football club is still one of the main ways in which working-class men – and increasingly women – make new friends when they move to a new town or city. No one cares if you are the life of the party, or a quietly reserved type when you try out at a new club. They only want to know if you can play – the social niceties can come later. And football can also be a way of keeping up ties with the place you have left behind.

JW: This level of local football can be an excuse for a drink after the match or even for continuing where you may have left off the night before. Money is largely removed. There may be some 'expenses' paid to the star players, but mostly *they* pay to play and they are mindful of sorting out their own fines for bookings or for getting sent off. At this grassroots level you can hope for the odd local newspaper headline, but there are few media spats between players and managers, or discord between the fans and the team. There is a closeness for everyone present – even the referee might get a hot cup of tea now and then.

SRC: So, there's you, from 'the village' or a small town maybe up north, someone who hates the game and all

'Preparing For The Match' - Hathersage, 2015
(SRC)

that village team niceness. And then you move to London, perhaps with a sense of relief or escape. But, lo and behold, you're soon dragged along to watch, or to be part of, the very thing you thought you had left behind!

JW: It can happen. And yet, for all this – for all the positive values local football can command – eleven-a-side grassroots football tends to struggle to recruit today. Shorter versions of the game, played under lights on midweek evenings, fit in better now with most people's busy lifestyles.

SRC: Today's local teams are a bit divorced from the old lineups that stare back at you in clubhouses, local bars, home mantelpieces, or in the local library. But at the FA HQ at St. Georges Park – which is about 180 miles from Ullswater in the Lake District – I had a chance encounter with one of the FA's marketing assistants. He told me that he dashes 'home' to Ullswater 'every once in a while' to keep goal for the club. I can appreciate anyone who wants to play for a village side, however irregularly. A warming story.

JW: Playing for your local place still means something. But as the traditional men's game goes downhill in its grassroots settings today, so there is one section of the football family that seems to be thriving. Local football for women and girls seems to be powering on…

CHAPTER 13

Women On The Side

'England Selfie' - St. George's Park, 2014
(SRC)

SRC: So, we have established that most young men want to do other things today rather than play local eleven-a-side football on muddied fields. They want to be with their families, go fishing, watch sports on TV, and so on.

Young women were never really encouraged to play sports at all. Then, about 100 years ago, they started playing football – and were good at it. This lasted about five or six years and then they didn't really play the game for another fifty years. But now they play again. It looks like they might be here to stay this time. Perhaps.

JW: That pretty much sums up matters. When the First World War broke out, British women from all kinds of backgrounds were ushered into munitions factories to do their patriotic duty. These women set up football clubs for leisure and to make money for the war effort, and they drew large crowds to their matches. The Dick and Kerr Ladies FC from Preston were the stars, an early women's club that even went on international tours and represented England. After the war, the FA was concerned that the female game might obstruct men's football, so

now the patriotic duty of women was to give up work and football and return to their homes. When they refused, in 1921 the FA cooked up a charge that the funds raised in women's charity games were being misused. The upshot was that women were banned from playing at all grounds of FA registered clubs – which meant almost fifty years of potential development lost. Outcasts, a handful of women's clubs in England then went underground until the 1960s, when the England male World Cup win – and feminism – inspired a new generation of female players.

SRC: I can't help feeling that, throughout football's history in Britain, women have periodically scrambled out of the box with the ribbon on it, and then been put back in it. They have been used mainly to titillate the men's scene. The old male order, feeling threatened or something else, snaps the box shut. The 'meet the wife' mentality rules once more. 'Meet the husband' would be equally annoying and demeaning, of course, if the roles were ever reversed.

JW: Unlike in the US – in fact quite the opposite – women in Britain have had to fight for the right to play from the very start. At least now most of the major men's clubs in England have developed and started to support women's teams. Manchester United were slow off the blocks for whatever reason – perhaps they were waiting to do it spectacularly in 2018 when it looked like they weren't going to do it at all.

SRC: So, there is a chance again for women in Britain to put their football boots back on. Whether or not they can get a foothold on the main pitch remains to be seen. There are still very few towns or cities in the UK where the women's club is better known than the men's club. Women don't represent places in football in the same

World War I - the stands of Tottenham Hotspur football ground have been turned into a workshop making gas masks, helmets, and other protective equipment for the war effort. The work of women, July 1916
(Mirrorpix)

way as men's teams do, and thereby they don't claim the ground. A few female clubs have shared stadiums with the men, such as Chichester City Ladies FC, but mostly, women play elsewhere: at sports centers, local schools, in the park, or even out of town. The women's team at mighty Liverpool FC once had to be content with playing matches at the home of the Widnes Vikings, a rugby league club from outside the city. What a poke in the eye.

JW: Your photograph of the Manchester City player injured against Liverpool at the 'Home of the Vikings' could have been taken at any game, male or female. But notice there is no phalanx of doctors and trainers in attendance here; injury in the women's game can be a lonely business.

It also demonstrates beautifully the physicality of women's football and the courage and resilience of female players after all those years when medical experts were regularly being wheeled out to tell us that women should not play sports at all because their bodies weren't up to it.

SRC: I never quite fathomed how I was always keen to flag up women's involvement in the male game, but initially I wasn't drawn to photographing women playing their own game. Then I realized why. It was because the women's game had no home; their clubs did not represent the town in a way that a men's club is seen as the club of the town. You never see graffiti about a women's club. Women had no football history in the UK, at least not one that we could

'One In The Eye For The Team' - Manchester City Women, 2014
(SRC)

easily talk about. When women played, it was regarded as just an anomaly. It didn't matter who won, where they played, and that there weren't any crowds to speak of. I've got over this now.

JW: The important thing is that women want their game to be considered on its own terms. They don't want it to be endlessly compared with the male game and there is no great push from female players to play alongside men. The top women in England have recently been professionalized in the Women's Super League, though their contracts are still tiny when compared to the top men. Given the more extensive TV coverage for women's football today, I guess young girls now have some role models they can look up to. For the first time it is entirely possible for young girls in Britain to fantasize about having a career in women's football, which is a major step forward. Let's just hope that professionalism doesn't mean that some of the bad habits of the men's game intrude too much into the women's equivalent.

SRC: The artistry in the women's game, and how it has no cheating – okay, less cheating – than men's football has me as a convert. Maybe one day women will get their own homes and maybe they will represent the local town. There has been a recent defrosting here of the habit of keeping males and females apart, encouraged by the supreme power of the FA. Now, year on year, the FA raises the age when males and females can take to the same field – even if they are not quite all leaping into the hot tub together later. I also see more women officiating at both men's and women's games in Britain. There are even some

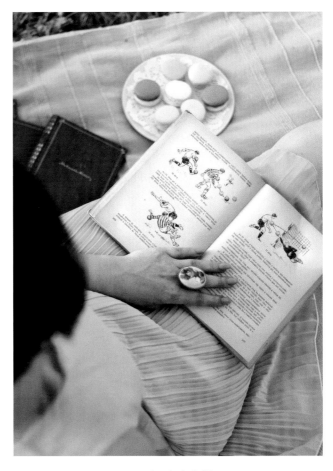

Woman reading the football laws,
by Szabados-Mavrák Norbert

women in power – or softish power – at the boardroom level of top male clubs. Karren Brady, chief executive at West Ham United, has a profile.

JW: Why no top female coaches – why does the women's national team in England have a male coach? Did you know that eleven of the last twelve major international tournaments for women have been won by a female coach? Go figure.

Your photographs usually tell us that females in the male game in Britain have typically been confined to the kitchens or the back rooms, are poorly paid, and are not key decision-makers. Some powerful men in football still seem to see women as little more than support workers or even childminders. In France in 2014, female ex-player Corinne Diacre became the first woman to coach a professional men's club. She now coaches the French women's national team, one of the strongest in the world.

'Mother And Son Man The Tea Bar' - Clydebank, 1995
(SRC)

Could a woman manage a professional male club here – why not? We have a long way to go, though – that fifty-year FA ban has really cost us.

SRC: British women have not been given an executive space in the football club car park because men think that they are the real drivers. Down the years, it has been presumed that most women don't really get the game. And certainly not the offside law. It was as if understanding that single law somehow defined who could become the footballing Doctor Who and who would become his [female] assistant. *Note: we now do have a female Doctor on the BBC at last.* A recent grassroots campaign, *This Girl Can*, run by Sport England, was much more positive and

'Heading Practice' - City Of Football Campaign, Nottingham, 2016
(SRC)

was a runaway success – including encouraging girls to play football. I worked on the project in Nottingham. It has been winning new hearts and minds, as well as awards.

JW: Girls and their parents are much more assertive today about their right to play the game. No more pleading with the sport's authorities and no more acceptance of casual sexism seems to be slowly edging up football's agenda. The shirts worn by Cheltenham Ladies FC bearing the slogan *No More Page Three* [the 'newspaper' showed a daily nude] are a brilliant and brave piece of sporting gender politics for the new century, don't you think? There is still some way to go, of course.

The LGBTQ community in Britain still gets a raw deal in football and there is no sign yet of a senior gay professional

Elaine, nineteen, had to nominate a goal-scorer who would net her an additional £200 per goal for every goal scored in a certain period. She chose Pop Robson of West Ham, 1973
(Mirrorpix)

in the men's game who feels comfortable and secure enough to come out. England women's captain Casey Stoney showed the way in 2014 when she spoke publicly about her female partner. Some fans - women as well as men - still see gender and sexuality as battlegrounds on which traditional attitudes have to prevail at all cost. Things will change, but only eventually.

'Three Lionesses' - England Women, 2014
(SRC)

SRC: One of the most remarkable recent steps taken by any club in Britain aimed at leveling the gender playing field has been at Lewes FC (est. 1885), who recently rebranded themselves as 'Equality FC.' Lewes is in a small, radical nonconformist pocket enclave of Sussex, just inland of Brighton, so you might expect something innovative here. In 2017 the local club introduced a policy of same pay for their men's and women's teams. They are also given equal access to the club's famous Dripping Pan ground. A smart marketing move – Lewes had loads of positive media coverage – but it may also be a statement about the future direction of travel for British football.

JW: Fair play to them. The women's game here seems

to be in a really strong moment, demonstrated by your remarkable photograph of those three England international players. What determination and strength of character is revealed here. The looks on these players' faces say to me: 'We have been through stuff, but now you need to take us seriously because we are powerful and we are not going away.' I think we are all beginning to get that message at last. And if I had to place a bet on it, I would say that England's best chance of winning a World Cup or a Euro title in the near future definitely rests with women like these. And who could say that, after the struggles they have come through and the barriers they have faced, they don't deserve it?

CHAPTER 14

The George, Best, and Barney Effect

SRC: When George Best was in his pomp in the late 1960s and early 1970s, routing the opposition single-handed on the football field by day and then going on an almost unbelievable dribble through the swinging-sixties landscape of Manchester by night, he completely changed our ideas about football, celebrity, and what it meant to be young. He was the best player I ever saw, for all kinds of reasons – and probably the first British footballer to act sexy and look truly young. Gone was the postwar monochrome era where you looked at photos of top players who already looked like old men. Those guys looked either too stiff, too pasty, or simply too old to play a thrilling, modern game. George turned all of that on its head, connecting rebellious youth culture to football.

JW: He was electric and irresistible. But just a few years after Northern Ireland's tricky George emerged replete with his fashion, cars, and girls, another significant footballing Best had also started the process of transforming the British game. His was a very different story.

Clyde Best was a Bermudan, and one of the first black players to resonate in the late sixties in England with young pretenders as well as antagonists. Clyde took some serious racist stick – even from his own 'supporters' at West Ham. 'I was like a fly in the milk,' he would say later about being pretty much the only black footballer playing regularly in the English First Division, and an irritant to terrace traditionalists. But he bedded in and got his admirers.

SRC: He must have had real courage playing at that time, a lone black beacon. These days you might examine any major club that had no black players. Quiet Clyde B. never complained about the terrible treatment he often received.

Clyde Best at Upton Park, March 1970
(Mirrorpix)

JW: It's true; black players were expected to take it all. Accepting racist abuse without complaint was often seen by their coaches and teammates as a kind of character test. He just had to suck it up, including even in the dressing room and on the training pitch. In August 1969, aged eighteen, Clyde was ready to take on Arsenal at Upton Park, and a few weeks after this debut he scored his first West Ham goal (out of forty-seven), against Halifax Town. Young black footballers in the UK can look back now at Clyde Best as one of the first guys to face racism inside the game and from opposing fans. British football supporters at the time seemed happy to purr and eulogize over famous international black players, such as Eusébio and Pelé, but these were black celebrities from over there.

Manchester United's George Best in the FA Cup fifth-round match at Northampton
Town, which United won 8-2, with Best scoring six, February 1970
(Mirrorpix)

Back here it was a different story. Those fans who did want to oppose racism were even prevented by the FA and the Football League from launching their own campaigns to support black players. The authorities called this 'bringing politics into football.' Clyde simply soldiered on alone.

SRC: Two great football Bests, but living in different worlds. George, like Clyde, came from across the sea, albeit from nearby Belfast. He nearly returned there before his professional football career had really begun. George had his adventurous streak but, like Clyde, he was actually a shy boy – a lad tied to the Cregagh Estate. Had his early homesickness at Manchester United gotten the better of him, we might have had a very different experience of the

revolution he helped usher in. You could argue, I suppose, that George's celebrity lifestyle and TV image in a way set out a marker for the global celebrity players who followed at Old Trafford, David Beckham and Cristiano Ronaldo. But, in the end, George found it just too much like hard work to keep his mad life on the rails. He was George Best on the pitch but for the tabloids and his drinking mates he was 'Bestie' off it.

JW: 'I was born with a great gift,' George said after his early retirement from the game, 'and sometimes with that comes a destructive streak. Just as I wanted to outdo everyone when I played, I had to outdo everyone when we were out on the town.' You did it, George. Early on, like

George Best with Miss United Kingdom, October 1966
(Mirrorpix)

lots of other players, Bestie could get wrecked on a night out without it being splashed all over the news headlines. But when he started to miss training sessions that was harder to keep quiet. Later, in the age of saturation TV football coverage, social media, and mobile phones, the game would become increasingly like a soap opera, with top players' social lives being endlessly picked over and exposed by the press, radio, TV, and social media alike. Any real privacy or discretion for elite footballers in England is now pretty much over.

SRC: Don't you think Sky TV would have begged for a George Best, or a Gazza? Mind you, the drinking culture of English clubs has waned since George and Paul Gascoigne did their thing. New diets and a generation of foreign players and coaches have seen to that.

But the satellite companies have done pretty well out of the deals with the Premier League since 1992. In George's and Clyde's time, the modest TV income was split between all ninety-two Football League clubs. The newly minted TV rights money today is gobbled up by the top twenty and its players and agents, meaning today's footballers are uber-handsomely paid and a lot of them have a global profile, not just UK domestic interest. Even

George Best did not get rich playing football.

JW: The TV money has also brought in these foreign stars, blocking some 'homegrown' talent. When only three out of ten Premier League players are qualified to play for England, you begin to wonder if the English club game has throttled the national team. But without Sky and BT Sport there is no way that British football could be quite so muscular globally and manage to put its content way ahead of that from all other countries. No one can question the commercial success of the Premier League and the power of its worldwide brand. Even British prime ministers hold it up as one of our great UK business success stories in the age of global deregulation. But at what cost?

By the midpoint in the season we now expect most managers in the bottom half of the Premier League will already have been sacked. We also expect some ambitious clubs in the Championship to spend much more than they can really afford to try to get promoted – and that some of them will crash and burn if they fail the test.

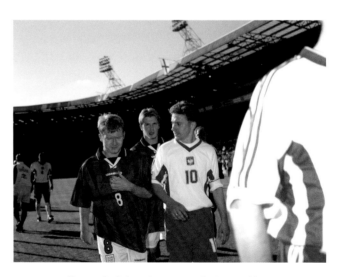

'Beckham And Scholes Before Him' - **England at Wembley, 1999**
(SRC)

SRC: It's like the song: 'You're just too good to be true, can't take my eyes off you – pardon the way that I stare, there's nothing else to compare' (Frankie Valli as of The Four Seasons). Lots of people these days say about the Premier League: 'I don't really like it – the greed, the transfer fees and wage excesses' – but I just can't resist it. Personally, I love it. I absolutely *love* it – like I love chocolate. But is it good for me, all this chocolate, and if I have too much of it will it make me feel just sickly?

JW: Chocoholic, you? I may be old-fashioned, but I'm just saying that top football today is cash-driven and is a product made more for TV than for the people who attend matches or for local communities.

Now VAR has arrived – video-assisted referee – we can really see how television has shaped the game. Referees can use VAR to help make decisions on offsides, penalties, and goals scored. The Americans have had the facility for some time in the NFL, but they use it sparingly. In any case, the NFL is played in chunks of time whereas our football is supposed to be continuous play. Now we have some guy drawing lines and taking minutes, with TV viewers, to look at a screen to decide if some player's armpit is offside. Meanwhile the fans at the game have no idea what is going on. Can you even celebrate a goal that VAR might rule out? Most fans - and players - seem to prefer leaving it in the hands of the match officials to these painstaking

judgments. We all know that VAR is really there to add value for TV viewers, football's new customers. Key people outside the game have shaped football's present format and will probably dictate its future.

SRC: It's men like Vic Wakeling and Barney Francis at Sky Sports we're talking about here, the men who pushed the current game well beyond the horizons of old-school club directors and the grassroots heartland.

In an indirect and roundabout way, my own family may have played a small hand in this. Back in the early 1980s my brother founded Berkhamsted Eagles FC. These boys had *nirvana* in local football terms: rarely scraping for kit and funds, a flotilla of doting parents offering transport to away matches, chocolate bars at halftime, and a rich social calendar off the pitch. The captain of one of these Eagles' sides became Sky Sports' guru Barney Francis, the man who in 2016 shook hands with the Premier League executive on a TV deal worth a mind-numbing £5.14 billion. Small world, eh?

CHAPTER 15

The Big Match Of The Day

The entire array of FA Cup entrants 2019-20,
prior to the Preliminary Rounds which start in August
(Courtesy of FA Cup Fact File)

SRC: Even in this amazing new Premier League era when live TV football rules, we still have, tiptoeing through this period, BBC's *Match of the Day* – event TV – everyone watches it. The choice match highlights of the day. This was the way we all used to receive the game on TV - extended highlights of selected games, covered by the BBC and also delivered in *The Big Match* show on ITV.

JW: They are showing repeats of *The Big Match* now on BT. Three things strike you right away: the terrible state of the pitches in the 1980s; how slow and unathletic the game seems compared to today's quick-fire, skill-rich football; and the fact that those old football TV programs were not dominated by repeat appearances of a handful of big clubs.

The entire array of Women's FA Cup entrants 2019-20,
prior to the Preliminary Rounds which start in August
(Courtesy of FA Cup Fact File)

SRC: Today, when the BBC or ITV [terrestrial TV free-for-all] cover an FA Cup game live – they still get very large audiences, even if smaller clubs are involved. Because somehow it is the national community watching football again, wanting a David and Goliath chapter from the football bible. It is not just those people who are star-gazing and who can afford to have satellite subscriptions.

JW: I think that's an important point. Watching football on TV was once, somehow, a communal demonstration of what you shared with other people, a kind of civic ritual as a citizen, rather than a signal about whether you were able to afford to buy access to the game, watched with a select few.

SRC: In 2020, you can watch live pretty much any match you like now on TV. It's all about choice – if you have the money. But choosing too much processed food will soon do you in. And the single-most popular football program

on TV is still *Match of the Day*, even though it is on at an awkward time and you can often be falling asleep on a Saturday night trying to stay up to watch it. The wholesome Gary Lineker still hosts. On *Match of the Day* the message always seems to be: you should watch this, because this is really *good* for you.

JW: It is officially the longest-running football TV program in the world. *MOTD* began in 1964 in black and white and it has managed to hold its place in the schedules regularly ever since, because people negotiating the TV deals for the Premier League realized that they also need access to the national audience for football, to try to keep the game alive in every household.

SRC: The really big 'live' football TV moments of my childhood were usually around the FA Cup because, for me, the cup was a tale about the nation. It was like the Grand National horse race of football. Everybody could

Destination Wembley. Fulham supporters on the way to see their team
take part in THE game of the season, the 1975 FA Cup final
(Mirrorpix)

enter and then the last two clubs left standing made it to the final at Wembley and everyone sat in front of the telly and applauded them. It felt like the whole country stopped to watch the FA Cup final at 3 p.m. on a Saturday afternoon in May. It ended the football season and waved in the cricketers. The FA Cup always represented the gallant side of the game, with great sportsmanship, excited kids in the crowd, giant-killings, and players politely applauding their opponents off the pitch.

JW: The oldest cup competition in the world, and it can still thrill today. The FA Cup was the first really national competition in England, because the Football League was initially dominated by clubs from the north and midlands.

So, winning the cup became a focal point for many clubs and a welcome counter to the marathon slog required in the league. It took Liverpool FC seventy-three years to win it. However, top clubs use the FA Cup today to rest players for the greater struggles ahead: for the Champions League or staying in the Premier League, where the big money is.

SRC: Since the FA Cup has become 'devalued,' I really think there may be a case for saying now that all clubs should enter at the same stage – the first week of August, just after the round of summer friendlies – and see who gets to Wembley in May.

Who knows, the giants could meet preposterously small football clubs before they have even properly

The Graf Zeppelin passing low over Wembley during the FA Cup final of 1930 in which Arsenal beat Huddersfield Town. The German airship, longer than the pitch, was booed by some of the crowd who thought it an uninvited distraction.
(Mirrorpix)

Close season, 1934.
The nine-foot-high cockerel, which sits above the stands at Tottenham Hotspur's White Hart Lane home, being cleaned whilst other ground improvements are made.
(Getty Images)

awoken to the new season. They could be giant-slayed on a sloping ground – or one where the corner is higher than the height of the goal crossbar (as at Heathwaite FC's pitch besides Lake Windermere). What fun! So British!

JW: I admire your romance and ambition, but the bigger clubs would cry foul very loudly about this crazy idea. They complain already that they play too many matches, and having Premier League clubs at really small grounds in August would be a security nightmare. We would also lose the aura of the third round, always the first week in the new year, when the big boys get thrown in and the surviving minnows start to dream. The FA Cup seems likely now to become a midweek, no-replay competition. More history lost. But we should stop hawking the TV rights to the draw to the highest bidder. Can't we get back to making sure that everyone has at least *played* before the next-round draw is made?

SRC: And another thing: Wembley Stadium should always be owned by the English game as well as being used for the FA Cup final only. I don't want it to end up being a home for American football.

JW: I understand your fears about selling off our best silver but you have to show a little flexibility. Holding the Football League playoffs and the various trophy matches at Wembley has really democratized the place, and has given lots of fans of smaller clubs a fantastic experience. Doesn't every football fan, no matter their level, deserve at least one day in the sun as invited guests?

SRC: We are talking about what makes the nation here – period – not just 'one day in the sun.' And in any case, it sometimes rains. This is England.

CHAPTER 16

The Show Must Go On

Valley Parade fire, Bradford City - sweeping through the mainstand in the five minutes before halftime, May 1985
(Mirrorpix)

Old Trafford suffers a direct hit - the most extensive damage suffered by any league club during the war, March 1941
(Mirrorpix)

JW: Historically, the game in Britain has been very slow-moving; we both know that. Clubs don't like change, fans don't like change. Most of the disasters in British football have actually come about because the game has refused to modernize, has been idle in looking to the future and in caring properly for its supporters. And yet, these are also some of the moments when British football has been forced to gather itself and change quite radically. This applies especially following that sequence of terrible tragedies that hit the British game in the 1980s, including the horrific fire in the Bradford City stadium in 1985.

SRC: The tough, rough 1980s with a series of fatal disasters were heartbreaking; I for one started to care deeply about the game. But I would concede that the game in this country has always been subject to interruption, going right back to the start. Two world wars – you can't get bigger interruptions than that. Football

in Britain has often been faced with having to pick itself up and start again. Bramall Lane – home for football and cricket – was bombed, so Sheffield United had to play at Hillsborough (home of their rivals). Old Trafford was bombed and Manchester United played at Maine Road (home of their rivals). Ironically, in February 1985 a match was postponed at Bramall Lane because an unexploded German bomb was found nearby.

JW: In the initial stages of the First World War, the game's authorities in Britain refused to follow the lead of the amateur Rugby Football Union to stop playing matches. The administrators in football argued that it was better to keep professional leagues going to maintain the morale of the people back home. 'It will all be over by Christmas' sort of thing. This was a very reasonable position to take but, of course, footballers and football people were criticized in the national press for being unpatriotic. While private-school-educated army officers were kicking and chasing a football into some muddied deathtrap of a no-man's land in France, working-class professional football players were lording it in safety back home. This was the story. A lot of it was simple class prejudice. Eventually the football authorities gave in.

Gravesend and Northfleet prepare for Sunderland
in the FA Cup, February 1963
(Mirrorpix)

Liverpool v Spurs at Anfield. Bob Paisley carries
off his injured skipper, Emlyn Hughes, April 1968
(Mirrorpix)

SRC: During the Second World War, players and fans were scattered all over the place. Turning up at grounds and makeshift matches they could never have imagined a few years before. There were plenty of players guesting at other clubs, depending on where they were based in the forces, so there was some continuity there. A little bit of pleasure in these extraordinary times. But these elongated interruptions must have been dulling and totally debilitating and were very different from the other thing that we really love contending with in Britain, and that's the weather. That's all part of it, football's winter tale. Try to get your pitch fit, whatever the skies throw at you.

JW: A lot of great British footballers lost the key years of their career because of war and, inevitably, a number of them did not come home. The 17th [Service] Battalion, Middlesex Regiment, was formed as a Pals battalion during the Great War, with a core group of professional footballers – the Footballer's Battalion. The Liverpool and England international Tom Cooper died serving for the Royal Military Police in 1940.

SRC: When league football finally resumed after the interruption of war, with all that horrible death and destruction, football was THE place to get folk back together again: a cheapish thrill. All that singing and supporting, shoulder to shoulder, without a real enemy. Is that why football in Britain was so popular in the late 1940s? People putting damaged lives and communities back together. These turned out to be the peak years through the turnstiles: the highest attendances ever across the country. Football crowds in Britain then eased off in the 1950s and 1960s, presumably because people found other things to do, the consumer society and all that.

JW: Football was so popular immediately after the Second World War because there really wasn't very much for working-class people to do in Britain. Football, the pub, the dance hall, and the pictures were basically it. Some cities were really badly damaged by bombing, and going to the game for men offered both an escape from the privations of the war years and a comforting return to some kind of normality. As Britain slowly recovered and wages for working people improved, so some fans did find other interests around new forms of consumption – DIY, home leisure, family outings, sports on television. Some younger supporters also began making a nuisance of themselves at the match. The local football club was no longer the automatic Saturday-afternoon outing for respectable working men and their mates. Wives and girlfriends wanted some leisure time too.

SRC: It was a place where men could become embedded, lose themselves. The mantra that 'The show must go on' is always around in football and it's quite a blokey thing of rolling up the sleeves and jumping into the cockpit of a digger that goes 'rat-tat-tat.' 'We must mend the pipes today' or 'Fix the floodlights.' No matter the state of the ground, the snow, or the floods, the view of the office staff and the groundsman is always: 'We'll get this game on!' Even Bill Shankly learned how to shovel snow. For the trainer, the spongeman, it's: 'Get the injured guy off the field, by whatever means, and then get him back on.'

I think solving national problems begins with the kind of resilience shown in small incidents in sports at the local level.

JW: Fair point. But postwar players were not really that well looked after in this respect. Photographs of players being carried off on the back of trainers also tells us something about the condition of British football. Few clubs had qualified medical staff and players often feared the treatment table. Before substitutes were allowed in league football in Britain [1965], injured men were usually made to return to the fray in order to add nuisance value, even if they could barely walk. Bert Trautmann broke his neck in the 1956 FA Cup final and played on. In the 1965 final – just before substitutes were allowed – the Liverpool defender Gerry Byrne broke his collarbone early in the game, but he kept his counsel and played on. Both City and Liverpool won.

SRC: Players were hard nuts in those days. So, the biggest off-field interruptions were the two wars, weather, and I guess you could also say the recession in the 1930s had an effect. But I know I'm right in saying that something which also had a huge impact on attendances later on was the Heysel disaster in 1985 and then what happened at Hillsborough.

The Liverpool manager, Bill Shankly, helps clear Anfield, Christmas 1964
(Mirrorpix)

JW: Heysel – where English hooliganism inadvertently led to the deaths of 39 Italian fans who were crushed when a wall collapsed before a European Cup final – had more of an impact than Hillsborough, I think. Heysel was definitely the lowest postwar point in English football in terms of image, public reactions to the sport, and falling crowds. Aggregate league attendances in 1948/49 were over 41 million; the season after Heysel they were down to just 16.5 million, and the game was also weighed down by some terrible newspaper headlines. I think a lot of people just gave up on English football at that point, had had enough of the fan violence and the awful facilities.

But modernization had already begun. The play-offs were introduced in England in 1986/87, signalling a greater understanding that most people now expected more than simply watching their local club playing out relatively meaningless end-of-season fixtures. The play-offs helped make football matter to more fans and to a new generation of supporters. By the time Hillsborough happened, football crowds in England were already on the rise. The show was slowly getting back on the road.

SRC: The Taylor Report, after Hillsborough, was also important here because Lord Justice Taylor basically talked about who we are as a people, why football was important to us. He discussed what we, the nation, wanted – and had a right to expect – from the game. He helped map out a new road to recovery.

JW: Lord Justice Taylor knew that the government at that time didn't really care about football or about the people

'The Day After Xmas Encounter' - Hillsborough, Sheffield Wednesday v Wolves, 1990
(SRC)

who watched it. To these politicians, football in England was just an embarrassment, a repeating policy problem. But Taylor listened to fans and wondered aloud why the sport was being so badly managed and why supporters who cared so much about the game were not being treated like customers – a dirty word to a lot of fans.

Taylor at least understood something about why football mattered so much to so many people and that it needed a radical shift to thrive. He wanted better and safer facilities (which he saw as seats) and a better general treatment for supporters, but also a change in attitudes. He was trying to drag the game, kicking and screaming, towards the twenty-first century. His report, plus the entrepreneurial ambitions of the men who wanted to lead football post-Hillsborough, plus the economic problems of satellite TV, all coalesced in the early 1990s. And out popped the Premier League in 1992!

SRC: A whole new ball game, no less. The other way we get the message, loud and clear from British football, that 'The show must go on' is when we think about how few clubs have actually been allowed to completely disappear, no matter the disasters, their financial problems, or their low levels of active support.

There is a real sense in the British game that, come what may, the local football club must somehow survive. Very few clubs in this country have bowed out completely. They are constantly being resurrected, with supporters' groups or local investors breathing dear life into their corpses. In a strange way, it seems that if your football club goes under then the place where you live somehow disappears with it. If war cannot destroy clubs then nothing else can.

CHAPTER 17

Football As Brand

SRC: So the Taylor Report offered a new direction for British football. But how did clubs respond to those big 'interruptions' we discussed in Chapter 16, especially the recent toll of tragedies? English football seemed to develop a new three-sided balance in the 1990s, between acknowledging fans as consumers (and so ensuring they got better treatment and more safety), promoting the glossy brand of Premier League football at the top, but also trying to hold on to a sense of football's great heritage as the authentic side of this equation. So the game is in this triangular balance now: consumer-brand-heritage. It means that all clubs should be able to hold on to the authentic element of their appeal and that smaller clubs have just about enough money coming in. But the game also recognizes that football, at some level, has to be a business.

JW: I think it is true that while some clubs really struggle financially, the game at the top level is trying hard to balance its business interests with sporting ones. Fans believe too often business wins out. But what constitutes 'authenticity' today is often very contentious for football supporters.

SRC: For fans at some clubs, coming out with a string of expletives, or having a proper row with rival supporters at a match, might be perfectly 'authentic' for them. My photograph of a wreck of a terrace at a Brighton versus Millwall playoff match at the old Goldstone Ground in 1991 sums this up.

There is a bit of a rivalry between these clubs and you might ask: where is all the crowd? Have they all gone home? In fact, the game is raging on somewhere below, out of sight. This young boy is being helped out through the broken pieces of a closed terrace by a first-aid man. It looks like the supporter has been hit on the head by a

brick or something.

To get the fan to somewhere safe, he has to be taken through what might, metaphorically, be regarded as English football's decaying past. It's meant to be a symbolic picture about the game on the edge of big changes. It is about where English football is trying to get to and the awkward steps it might still have to take to get there. And there may also be some displacement of the 'old guard' coming at this very moment, either because standing areas of grounds were being closed down – like here – or because clubs just didn't want a certain type of supporter anymore.

JW: This is a sharp reminder of aspects of 'the bad old days' and that safety would soon come high up on English football's new agenda. Fans at different clubs certainly do have their own ideas about what constitutes 'authenticity' and the club 'brand' – which is likely to be quite different from how most club owners see it. The songs that supporters sometimes sing about themselves, and about how fans of other clubs see them, is authentic for them, a key part of their identity. So, there can be a big difference between the official packaging of football today and how local people on the terraces and in the stands respond to the game. This can easily put some supporters at odds with the clubs they love. They might think that their own chief executive focuses far too much on the corporates, merchandise, and the store – but that is part of the new equation that you were just talking about.

SRC: The Goldstone Ground had seen better days, but the new Brighton stadium, the Amex, does feel to me like it's part of the community and that the club has opened itself up to all sorts of inclusive activity and support for local fan initiatives.

'Led Away Hurt' - The Goldstone Ground, Brighton and Hove Albion, 1991
(SRC)

JW: I know Brighton fans have been involved in progressive pro-LGBTQ campaigns which have been largely supported by the club. This might smack of 'new' football for some traditional fans but it is important. Brighton's story of being displaced, homeless, and then returning to the local area as a successful and responsible Premier League club in a very smart stadium is also an inspiring football tale for today.

SRC: How does authenticity work in a two-club city? Sheffield United and Sheffield Wednesday fans might have some minor differences about branding and what is authentic for them. Fans of both clubs might welcome investment from abroad, because it gives their club more chance of getting promoted and of getting one over on their local rivals. But on the day when these clubs meet, the song that will be booming out loudest from Sheffield United fans will be a very local one, which has a very local meaning, about 'a greasy chip butty.' These United fans have adapted a conventionally romantic ballad and made it a powerful and moving football anthem, but one that is only remotely romantic and meaningful to the supporters who sing it. And me.

JW: The point is, it almost doesn't matter what is happening, business-wise, to clubs like these when they meet. Whether one club has more global ambitions, or one has gone down the foreign investment route more than the other. The core meaning of that match to those supporters will be pretty much the same as it's always been. There is a kind of 'essence' of Sheffield United, which will always be playing an 'essence' of Sheffield Wednesday; a meeting full of all those memories of past encounters and how these two clubs identify in the city. 'Hark now hear the Wednesday sing' will be coming from the other side. Everything has changed, but everything also remains the same. People who are less connected to Sheffield, who may be watching this match on TV in distant parts of the world, will have a very different take on it, of course. They might ask out loud: 'I wonder where Sheffield is?' For them, it might just be another blue-and-white stripes versus red-and-white stripes. After all, until recently, global football fans even wondered where exactly Leicester City were based.

The changing hairstyles of David Beckham
(Courtesy of Ben Farr Illustration)

personality. Beckham became a global icon, someone whose image was no longer 'contained' by football, by Manchester United or by the Premier League itself. His haircuts were also monitored pretty much on a daily basis at one point. He became an industry in his own right – a cultural brand recognized all over the world, and not just because of football.

Some clubs, such as Leeds United, have a brand image that can somehow support as many as eleven different match-day scarves, expressing an unbelievable range of things that just don't seem to add up.

'Gingerbread On The Street' - Sheffield Wednesday v Sheffield United, 2012
(SRC)

SRC: Footballers from the past were brands in a sense, but very small brands. They often had to find another income. They ran a pub perhaps. Possibly not in the town where they made their name – and so the pub becomes a bit of a tourist attraction. Then players became bigger brands. In the internet age, someone like David Beckham became much less known for his heroic sporting character than for his commercial ambitions and his media-friendly

JW: I think this is a great photograph because it demonstrates so well both the enduring inventiveness and humor of football culture – though it's not always *that* funny – but also the new patterns of consumption developing around the game in the Premier League era. There are just so many potential football identities in play now, we are clearly beyond the age of, simply, following your local club and wearing its standard colors.

The game is so tied up today with the marketplace, with matters of consumption and catering for different styles of support and with offering choice about how you demonstrate your fandom. Working out how to access different fan constituencies is all part of increasing the appeal of the product. It is a message, I'm afraid, about how football is increasingly packaged, just like any other brand or cultural activity, to maximize its customer impact.

'To Decorate One's Self' - Leeds United, 2012
(SRC)

'Carrying The English Beckham Baby'
England v Brazil at Shizuoka, Japan, 2002
(SRC)

SRC: You could say that this sort of thing has kind of dissipated the one central push of what it means to be a fan of any club – or you could say it's expanded it. You can click on any of these channels and they will all bring you Leeds United, but each in a slightly different register.

JW: True. But once you get inside the stadium among your fellow Leeds supporters, then most people are still doing pretty much what they have always done: getting behind the club and experiencing that powerful and anonymizing sense of collective solidarity. Football, rather cleverly, still offers the traditional attraction of being involved in something much bigger than the individual – all in one community – but it has also responded to the individualizing impact and appeal of wider social changes. You can choose how you, as an individual, want to be seen to be a fan, while also blending into the home support when you want to feel a part of the crowd.

SRC: Standing out at football still seems important to some people. Most British football supporters will probably have an aversion to my photograph of this pair of England-Beckham supporters in Japan in 2002. It may be more offensive in a way, than the photograph of all those Leeds scarves. At international level, it's almost as if football can say that we can market the game in any way we like because there are more than 200 countries out there and they all have different tastes. The Russians,

hosts to World Cup 2018, and others may not like this 'English' style of 'family' supporting, but the Japanese do – they get 'kitty cute.'

JW: All the photographs in this chapter, taken together, tell us that there are so many different versions of iconic stars out there, so many brand options, and so many different ways of being a fan today, that you can connect with football in pretty much whatever way you like. Perhaps we need to be a little more tolerant of people who want to express their support for the game in these different ways, rather than laying down any hard-and-fast rules about 'authenticity' or what a 'real' fan looks like. We know that some fans will never be able to attend a match of the club they support, and that the global reach of the very large clubs in England can be tailored so that this doesn't impact too much on local fans.

All fans matter irrespective of the scarf they choose, or the baby they hold. Despite everything in the UK from 2016 onwards – including the Brexit we now face in 2020 – the football brand seems to ride out the major storms buffeting Britain. It is a brand that stretches across different leagues, geographies, and financial inequalities within the UK, where devotion and attendance hold true. It is the baby. It is the real McCoy. Even in the USA, home of baseball, the NBA, and the NFL, and where TV invariably appears to be a better way of receiving 'live' sports, soccer attendances are soaring.

CHAPTER 18

The Attendance Is Important

JW: In Britain, nothing in football can replace the thrill of being there. How could it? This British obsession with football attendance goes right back to the early years of the game. Aston Villa were getting crowds of 40,000 in 1903. Nottingham Forest could only attract 1,500 for the visit of Stoke City. Remember that 200,000-plus crowd that hustled into the first Wembley FA Cup final way back in 1923? And what about the 147,365 who were officially present for the 1937 Scottish Cup final between Celtic and Aberdeen at Hampden Park? Plenty more sneaked in. I think only the Brazilians and maybe the Portuguese, historically, come close to these sorts of figures. And even today the second tier, the Championship in England, draws higher aggregate attendances than the top leagues in France, Italy, and Spain. We truly love *going* to football here.

'The Gasheads Gaskets Tested' - **Bristol Rovers at Wycombe Wanderers, 2014**
(SRC)

SRC: Attendance can be as important to some football fans as the score. We always ask: How many came? Was the ground full? Did little Matlock Town get a crowd?

For all the pressures from the Sky and BT paymasters and for all the top-level focus on the global footprint of the Premier League, we all want some validation, to experience something special, by being able to say: 'I was there.' But how do we value attendance? Should a smaller Football League club be convinced that the drip-down payment (from Barney's Premier League TV deal) compensates for a home crowd of, say, 3,000 when they had budgeted on home matches bringing in 4,500-plus? But this is no real measure compared to the wider value of football at smaller clubs. Is an entire season at Grimsby, for example, with all the marvelous images and experiences it conjures up, really worth less than a lower-end Matisse painting? I don't think so.

JW: I hadn't expected that fine-art comparison. Let me try a different tack, to make a similar point. I read a story recently about a fan called Kitty Thorne, from Trowbridge, Wiltshire. Kitty used to head off on the midday steam train to the old Bristol Rovers ground with a packed lunch of corned beef sandwiches and a flask of tea to watch her club play. Her first match was in 1954 when she was close to forty, and she was still attending in 2018 at 103 years of age. How many honors did Rovers win in those sixty-four years? I can tell you that: a couple of playoff wins and a Third Division title in 1990. Kitty only had to wait thirty-six years for it. She was not going for the glory, that's for sure; something else kept her motivated. She was a bit like so-called 'superfan' Pete Moran.

Since November 10, 1987 – when Ronald Reagan was US president and Tiffany's 'I Think We're Alone Now' topped the UK pop charts – Pete has been to every one of Stoke City's matches, home or away. Just think about that for a second: illness, family events, holidays, weather, transport issues. Nothing stopped him getting to Stoke games.

'The Attendance Is In' - Matlock Town, 2014
(SRC)

SRC: Sometimes, you just have to admire – and maybe be slightly concerned about – the utter devotion of some supporters, no matter their age or the stature of the club they follow. The compulsion of attending matches shows that the game is much more than a mere hobby or entertainment. It gets in your blood.

JW: That's because for football supporters always 'being there' often restates something important about our identities and our place and family ties; about our loyalty to friends and to our club. But I think it can also say something about a collector's fetish and a deep-seated fear: what if something truly amazing happens and I'm not there? Those groundhoppers and people who never miss a game always seem to be men of a certain age. Some

people deride them as train-spotters – as anoraks.

SRC: Forget the turnstile cash – football means little to a TV audience if the ground isn't full, or close to it. 'Why should I bother watching on TV if this club has no fans of its own?' For me, someone who photographs ordinary football people and who sees their value as part of the fabric of the sport, seeing massed banks of fans also says something about the British values as a nation. I hope my photographs of fans add some value to football, reinforcing the message about why supporters who go to matches matter so much to the game.

JW: I remember that the AC Milan owner, Silvio Berlusconi, once said that if fans stopped attending

'Show Of Color' - Leicester City, 2013
(SRC)

because too much football was being shown on TV, clubs should pay them to come – as one might pay extras in a television spectacular.

Fortunately, we still appreciate our football clubs, not just for what they have achieved or how much money they are worth, or even the TV audiences they may get in China. We still look at how many people actually want to pay to watch them play. How many people express that irreducible commitment to the cause?

Look, we simply don't have that many public events these days where people from very different backgrounds and social classes can still sit or stand together and really share something significant in their lives as they do at football. Nobody in Britain thinks that a club such as Newcastle United, for example, is not important just because it has not had much recent success. We look instead at its history and the current attendance figures and marvel at northeast supporter loyalty and their belief that, one day, all this may change. We all know how important cases like Newcastle United are to the wider football narrative. And we all know how that club's supporters feel in their quarrels with owners.

SRC: And my quarrel with gallery curators was that they told me that football had no place in art galleries. I said, 'We shall see.' My show went on tour for an unbroken span of fifteen years – all at publicly funded art galleries. Is there anything as operatic and strangely beautiful as seeing a decked-out 50,000-strong football crowd sing its favorite anthem? The longest-running plays eventually come and go, but football never goes: it just keeps on

running. Football grounds are not usually officially listed for public protection, but virtually every football ground is revered in the sporting public's psyche. Our historic football grounds don't need a blue plaque to be valued by the fans who fill them.

JW: It is interesting that there are groups of football supporters in this country – usually middle-aged men – who like to visit the most obscure football places, to be present in some of the smallest football crowds, because they are collectors and they appreciate the quirkiness and the diversity of the live football experience. You can visit significant and attractive places in England, Scotland, Wales, and Northern Ireland by attending football. Some fans even write lyrical top-selling books about the camaraderie and the adventures in the game's lower reaches. Some supporters might insist on boasting about having 'been there' at some of the sport's biggest-ever fixtures – about half a million Englishmen claim to have been at Wembley on July 30, 1966 – but there are plenty more who will happily bend your ear in a pub about being among the 346 souls who traveled to Derbyshire in heavy drizzle for a mid-table non-league contest in an open field that barely drew a line of national press coverage.

SRC: I worry that this might be a specifically British male mentality; something that goes right back to ideas of drawbridge Britain, and 'the island' and sacred ground, and that 'No other should tread on this land than us.' At some moments I think it might be all that sort of inward-looking stuff that is going on here. And then I change my mind and think: what a wonderful way of wasting one's time, if that is indeed what it is.

JW: Consider this: in March 2019, Wrexham FC - historic Welsh exiles playing in the fifth tier of the English game, and around about the 100 mark in the list of all professional clubs in England and Wales – drew a crowd of 7,106 to watch a home match versus Chesterfield. A few days later 8,283 fans watched Wrexham play Salford City. These are quite remarkable levels of support. What else is there to do in Wrexham? you might ask [population around 150,000]. These crowds are larger than those at many clubs playing at the top level in some football leagues on the continent. We love our local football clubs in Britain and we turn out to support them, no matter how far they have fallen from grace.

CHAPTER 19

Foxes At 5000-1

SRC: We all know that in every season, and possibly every week, English football throws up wonderful stories. Blackpool; Huddersfield Town; Hull City; little homespun Barnsley, all at one time in the Premier League. Pull the other one! And then cue the street celebrations. And what about Burnley's return from disappearing up the Colne Valley? These are all great short stories in their own right.

But Leicester City actually winning the Premier League title in 2016 – well, that's a complete volume of fairy tales right there.

JW: I live in Leicester and my family are all City fans. We had journalists from all over the world descend on the place in 2016. The whole city was caught up in the narrative of that title season, wondering when the dream was ever going to end. To everyone's astonishment, it didn't.

SRC: We will get back to Leicester City later, but first can I mention an entire exhibition I made about just one game? We called it: 'May 13, 2012.' Manchester City gave me special access that day. They just rang me up and said: 'Please come along and capture what will hopefully be our happiest day for a long time.'

They were not bragging, or taking things for granted, but they wanted a record of what happened. All the gallows humor of the previous twenty years at Manchester City hovered over the stadium that afternoon.

City had to win against lowly QPR to secure the club's first title for forty-four years but, typical City…

The match didn't go to plan! The City fans were helpless, looking at their kids' faces for reassurance. No one knew quite what to do; the very life was draining out of them. And, worst of all, it was the club down the road, Manchester United, that was going to gain from this most colossal of all cock-ups.

'Bottoms Up' - Barnsley, 1997
(SRC)

I got myself between the City and QPR fans to capture both sets of fans' emotions, but I somehow knew I had to get to the end that City were attacking for the final few moments, even though it looked a lost cause. Call it a photographer's instinct.

Then, Edin Džeko scores a header and, with pandemonium breaking out all around, the great man Agüero slides in the winner. BOOM! I think I can even divide my work in football by that day – BC (Before City) and afterwards – because the experience on that one afternoon in Manchester just fried me and served me up all over again.

And, football, being football, you think you have really seen it all now, that there will never be another day quite like this one. I really should have known better. Just four years later, Leicester City took it to another level. They provided an answer to all those doubters and moaners in the bar who say that the game is 'just about money.'

JW: Approaching the run-in in 2016. I think everyone in Leicester knew that this was a once-in-a-lifetime opportunity for this club. The bookmakers certainly did: they had initially offered odds of 5000-1. You could get a better price on finding intelligent life on another planet. My own mother-in-law is a Leicester season-ticket holder in her eighties and I think she knew that her decades of loyal support and longing had been building up to this one, tantalizing moment. Four lost FA Cup finals, no league titles. Could the Foxes really hold it together at the last, hold their nerve?

Every conversation with non-fans in Leicester towards the end of the season seemed to begin: 'I don't normally like football, but...' The entire city was gripped, people from all sorts of ethnic and cultural corners felt involved. I think only football can do this, can bring people from all kinds of social backgrounds inside the community tent in a mass celebration of who we are. It can reach beyond the market and community boundaries. It still matters to people.

There was something indefinable – almost mystical – about *that* group of players, and *that* coach, and *that* crowd working in perfect harmony for a few months in Leicester. It reminded us all, I think, that in the twenty-first century, for all the money talk and ownership wrangles, for all the investment angles and the asset stripping and the massive player salaries, this is still a glorious, unpredictable sport, not simply a business. A man such as Jamie Vardy could still rise from a career in non-league football and a period

'Players Celebrating Promotion' - Leicester City, 2014
(SRC)

on a police-enforced electronic tag to be at home among these international thoroughbreds and to win a Premier League title medal. There is also a link with Manchester City because it was when Leicester City went to the Etihad in February 2016 that most pundits finally expected the visitors to crumble and fall away. Normal service would soon be resumed, most people said. Watch Manchester City crush this dream. Instead, the boys from Leicester puffed up their chests and destroyed their hosts. And the rest, as they say, is consigned to history – and its imagery.

SRC: I think there was this national feeling that Leicester had been a hare out of the traps and most people said: 'They will not keep that up. It is impossible that a club such as Leicester City will win the title.' They were proved wrong, of course. And what has been the value of that fact to the British game? In the era when money talks and accountants rule, here is a football club of modest means, but with great team spirit and some key players, turning the world of football upside down. If you could bottle it, the queue to buy would stretch for miles. Their title win added ten years on the life of the game. The year 2016 reminded all of us of why we watch the game at all. It gave every football supporter of every aspiring club, at any level in the game, a huge shot in the arm. The moral of this story is: you all matter and one day your time will come. God bless those fearless Foxes!

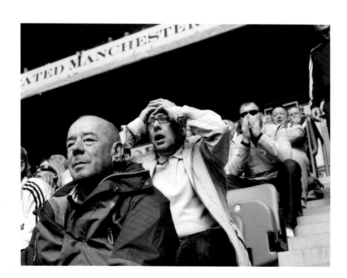

'Hands On Head At 1-2' - Manchester City, 2012
(SRC)

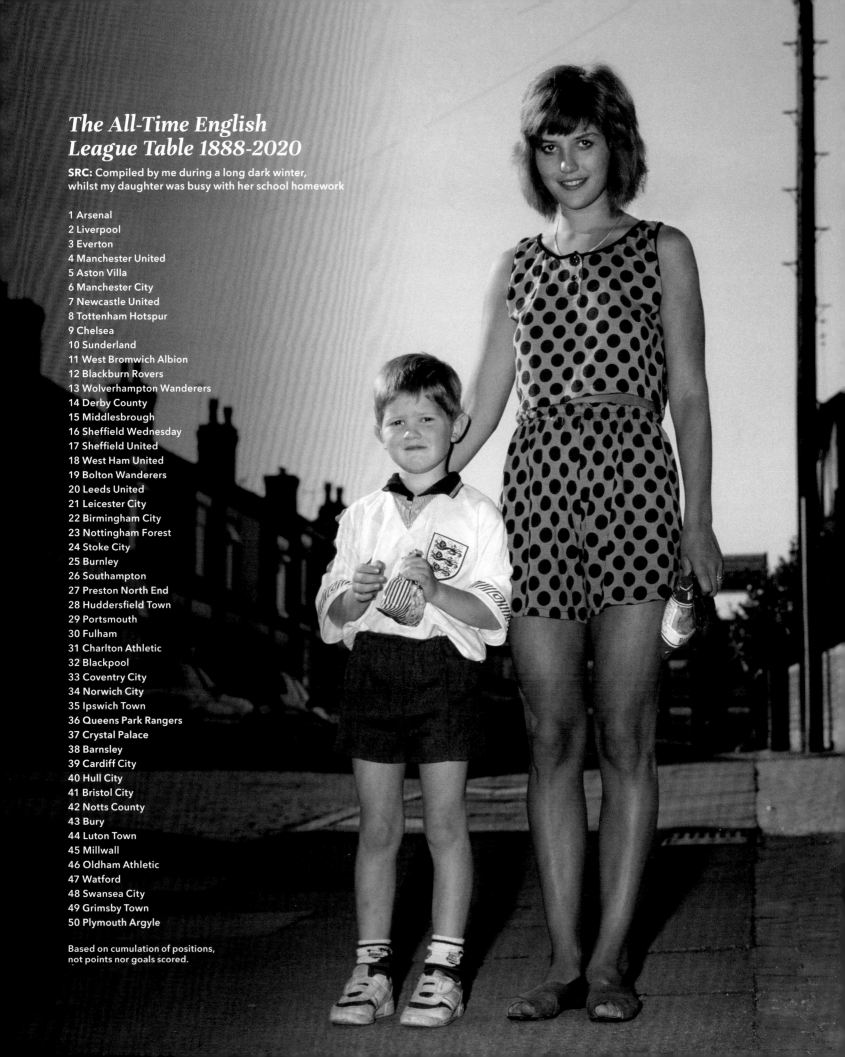

The All-Time English League Table 1888-2020

SRC: Compiled by me during a long dark winter, whilst my daughter was busy with her school homework

1 Arsenal
2 Liverpool
3 Everton
4 Manchester United
5 Aston Villa
6 Manchester City
7 Newcastle United
8 Tottenham Hotspur
9 Chelsea
10 Sunderland
11 West Bromwich Albion
12 Blackburn Rovers
13 Wolverhampton Wanderers
14 Derby County
15 Middlesbrough
16 Sheffield Wednesday
17 Sheffield United
18 West Ham United
19 Bolton Wanderers
20 Leeds United
21 Leicester City
22 Birmingham City
23 Nottingham Forest
24 Stoke City
25 Burnley
26 Southampton
27 Preston North End
28 Huddersfield Town
29 Portsmouth
30 Fulham
31 Charlton Athletic
32 Blackpool
33 Coventry City
34 Norwich City
35 Ipswich Town
36 Queens Park Rangers
37 Crystal Palace
38 Barnsley
39 Cardiff City
40 Hull City
41 Bristol City
42 Notts County
43 Bury
44 Luton Town
45 Millwall
46 Oldham Athletic
47 Watford
48 Swansea City
49 Grimsby Town
50 Plymouth Argyle

Based on cumulation of positions,
not points nor goals scored.

CHAPTER 20

There Will Always Be An England

'Worker Being Abused By England Fans' - Bologna, World Cup 1990
(SRC)

'England Fans Being Abused By Italian Police' - Bologna, World Cup 1990
(SRC)

SRC: I was given a luxury camper van by VW to do a road trip to the World Cup in Russia. The British government was saying DON'T GO and no one knew I was going. I HAD to go. Had to be there. I drove well over 10,000 miles to be there. Single-handedly. What a driver.

The UK I returned to seemed as alien as Russia and the countries in Europe I had traveled through. This totally took me by surprise. Over the span of thirty years I felt I had come to know my UK intimately through its football, its humor, weather, coast, and geography – and its sticking up for others. I had never really felt at home with, or understood at all, Margaret Thatcher, Mark Thatcher, pre-plane-crash Nigel Farage (he was almost killed), post-plane-crash Farage, the *Daily Mail*, The National Lottery UK, etc. Football, above everything else, was how I knew my country and why I began the Homes of Football. Attendances for domestic matches – league games – are still strong despite all the Brexit upheaval, despite everything. So there's something about being

there. When I am at the football I never wonder about who they voted for, which side in the referendum they were on. While they might be yelling their heads off in a partisan way, I think THEY ARE FOOTBALL FANS and that is enough for me. Because there's a sort of lore inside the domestic football ground.

But when it comes to supporting Eng-er-land, I approach it with a bit of caution, especially lately. In fact much like I did when I started all this off at the end of the 1980s. Have we come full circle?

JW: So, let's talk England-on-the-pitch. After recent performances in major competitions you might have got pretty decent odds on England winning the World Cup in Russia in 2018. Last major trophy in 1966 - ancient history. No wins in the group in Brazil in 2014 and then brought down by Iceland in the Euros in 2016. Iceland! Where, exactly, do you go from there? A new young English coach with a poor domestic club record and little international experience was the FA's answer.

SRC: Ahhh, but don't forget, we actually did quite well back in Italia 1990 under Bobby Robson. Gazza's tears and the way we outplayed Germany in the semifinal? I have a little human-interest story about Bobby Robson. This was a few years later and he had come to open one of my exhibitions. He was running late, so I asked the gallery manager where he was and he said: 'Bobby's driving around the block – he's a little nervous.' I said: 'Nervous? He's the ex-England manager!' He said: 'Yeah, but it's an art exhibition; it's not quite his territory.' I said: 'Get him in here; he'll be fine, a national hero.' And he comes in and he is very nervous. So I say that lots of people will want his autograph, and he can do those later. I then say: 'Come and have a look at these photographs,' and some of them are of England fans around 1990. That young woman in a polka dot dress standing with a lad in an England shirt [underlay of page 95]. He asks: 'Who is she?' Well, I didn't know. I just told him that while he was holed up in a hotel in Italy, people back here in England were going absolutely crazy: kids were staying up late wearing England shirts; big parties were happening; mums and daughters and sisters watching matches were becoming England fans, following Gary and Gazza. And now Bobby relaxes a little

'Gazza On National Service' - **England At Wembley, 1991**
(SRC)

and he starts talking to people. In the end, we couldn't get him out of the place. He really had no idea of the impact his team had on the country and the England 'brand.' With social media it is probably all very different today.

JW: I was at that World Cup in 1990 with England fans and it was a very weird experience. I started off in Milan and saw Cameroon beat the holders, Argentina, in the opening match. What a start! There was this amazing street party after the game involving what seemed like all the Africans who were based in Milan, the street traders and others. It was like a fabulous festival, bringing the whole African continent together but in Europe. This is what the World Cup is supposed to be about. Then, the next day I flew to Cagliari, where England were based. Basically, we had been confined to an island prison, away from all this party atmosphere. Thousands of police officers and press, a thoroughly miserable exercise.

SRC: The real low-bottoming-out point for England and UK football was in the mid-1980s. We mentioned Bradford and Heysel as tragic wake-up calls. Our England national football-supporting culture was shot through. In Scotland they fared a bit better – their Tartan army were a bit more loveable and so pleased to get to Mexico in 1986.

However, England fans were certainly turning things around after 1990, and by 1996 we had a head of steam on - England hosted the Euros and we had that 'Football's Coming Home' feel-good vibe, a new fusion between

The Cure's Robert Smith and Big Country's Stuart Adamson during World Cup, 1986
(Tom Sheehan)

music and football. No pop band worth its salt would now claim not to have a favorite football club. No football fan, nor any club, could refuse to turn to music to get an extra kick. Tony Blair was inviting anybody who was somebody to Downing Street for Prosecco. Eng-er-land was having a good time, but also showing much more tolerance of others. That sense of superiority and entitlement we once had was finally evaporating.

JW: By the early 2000s, we also began to see much more variation in the England traveling supporter; more women, some older fans, even BME England fans going abroad. The England Supporters Group started to isolate troublemakers and to promote a new version of football patriotism. Following England abroad began to feel more inclusive.

SRC: England's home base – accessible for all in the Midlands - eventually did come about, a decade postponed, when St. George's Park was opened in 2012. For me, that is the single major recent factor you can identify for why the national team started to do well again. All twenty-one England teams spend some time there, women as well as men, and youth teams. This place has facilities to match those anywhere in the world, but it's also pretty accessible. It's not massively security-conscious; people can wander about a bit. No guard dogs and sentries. Some trust. I think that is part of the English mentality; we quite like that. So, St. George's Park has that real sense of excellence and expertise, but it also feels very comfortable and really quite open.

JW: With the arrival of St. George's Park and discussions

'Valley Of St. George'
England v France At Lisbon, Euro 2004
(SRC)

about an 'England DNA,' it also felt like there was some kind of wider strategy in place for once: 'We don't expect to win the World Cup right now, but we are trying to build towards something better.' At least we had a structure now to hold on to for the future, and things certainly did feel a little more forward-looking.

SRC: That's true. We had to move on from Terry Butcher's 'blood and bandages' kind of Englishness. We may, from time to time in history, have to step back from the front of the stage for a while. This was one of those times.

JW: Now we had a plan. And we had a message, which the English public understood, about working with talented younger players, and that bringing them through will take time. We had to try to get away from the media hype that invariably followed England teams around. We were working towards a fresh new approach, no baggage, and we were going to work now with younger English coaches, because buying in hotshot mercenary coaches from abroad had simply not worked. How could they understand us, get the best out of English players?

SRC: The recent successes of Wales and Northern Ireland in international tournaments confirm that point. They have made the maximum out of their national playing base, and Wales certainly have great team spirit but also some world-class talent. Perhaps the tragedy of the loss of Gary Speed [page 119] also offered some inspiration here? Recent successes for England have probably been a little more calculated than those intuitive ones for Wales and Northern Ireland.

'A Nation's Homecoming' - Cardiff, Euro 2016
(SRC)

'England Fans v Wales' - Lens, Euro 2016
(SRC)

JW: That brings us nicely to the World Cup finals in Russia in 2018. Britain and Russia were hardly the best of diplomatic friends at this precise moment. Of course, Vladimir Putin was going to manage the World Cup finals to the last detail in order to squeeze every drop of positive coverage for his leadership. Most host countries do much the same. Quite predictably, local homophobia, racism, and hooliganism were effectively banished from the tournament under threat of severe state action.

SRC: When I eventually got to Russia in 2018, I found a few English journalists but I couldn't find any other England fans – none. But the South Americans were there in their tens of thousands. They were everywhere: Peruvians, Colombians, Argentinians, and Mexicans. In Russia! Sometimes you had to think to yourself: 'Is this really

happening?' It was a bit of a mad joyous dream where everything goes right and not wrong - and you wake up and stretch your toes and limbs and think the world is kind of furry. This is as good as it gets!

JW: The World Cup is becoming a bit of a TV spectacular, only, which is a real shame, because if you do manage to be there and get among an extreme clash of cultures – a Nigeria versus Iceland match or a Saudi Arabia versus Uruguay – it is a wonderful thing to be a part of. Whenever do countries like these get to sit at the same table, their peoples sharing a common bond and checking each other out?

SRC: When England played Wales in a rather scruffy French town, Lens, in the 2016 Euros, it was equal play.

'The Greatest Throng' - Moscow, World Cup 2018
(SRC)

'Watching England Through The Window' - Kaliningrad, World Cup 2018
(SRC)

'English Car At Nuremberg Campsite' - **World Cup 2006**
(SRC)

The English were not chucking things at the Welsh or wildly chasing them down the street. They were walking with each other to the stadium, like civilized fans on an equal footing, wanting to see their respective countries progress. In 2016 Russian fans were head-hunting and England were the prize. Strangely, in the eyes of the world we were suddenly the victims for once.

JW: It was odd watching the 2018 World Cup from England. Brexit implied nothing was working and as a nation we didn't seem to be going anywhere. And yet, here was a young England football team, with a very young manager (in a waistcoat), which had a real sense of purpose and togetherness. Here was a modern version of Englishness. The parents or grandparents of many of these England players had been migrants. Here was a progressive England, seemingly open and confident of its place in the world, while politicians squabbled over their own narrow, ideological interests. These young footballers in 2018 had a pride and a dignity in playing for their country and they were not weighed down by the shirt or by their national identity. Or Brexit.

SRC: They also looked fabulous, athletic, and toned. They were impeccably well-behaved. This was not what we were used to, given stories about Premier League players being rich before their time and lacking respect. As England started to have some success, I elected to go back home to see what was happening in England. I thought this was where the atmosphere would now be, that the whole

country would be going bonkers, like in 1990. But there was only politeness, a rather controlled interest. No one was buying into the media hype this time. Even outside, at the big screens, it was very reserved; people donning the Gareth Southgate waistcoat was about as wild as it got.

JW: There was not much of the xenophobic tabloid craziness we usually get around England and the World Cup. And people who wouldn't have identified in the past with England and football because of the behavior of some fans, the tabloid laddishness of the players, or the idiotic media focus on WAGS, could see something different here. I think that really struck a chord. We even had female ex-players on the TV coverage in England. They were not just attractive hosts or eye candy for male viewers. They were offering real punditry and smart analysis based on experience. Alex Scott featured a lot - 140 England caps. She knew exactly what she was talking about, and even if some male panelists tried to patronize her, she really wasn't having any of it. Here was another modern shift, a new gender attack to balance up the Talkbloke vibe.

'Crowd Watching The Big Match'
England v Croatia, Weymouth, World Cup 2018
(SRC)

SRC: I think these women are great role models for plenty of younger blokes. The guys were probably thinking, 'Well they're doing brilliantly, they carry themselves perfectly off the pitch and they are doing so well on it.' Those England women are great examples: hardworking, no cheating; no running to the press at any moment. Male or female, all ages, I have to say that the national team players do seem to have equal worth at St. George's Park at least – this being the home of the England teams, where roles are defined.

JW: So, is this a new era for England, with male and female teams and age squads developing in concert together? In fact, from nowhere we are suddenly in this incredible position where it's perfectly possible to think that both the male and female senior England teams – and half the junior teams to boot - might win international trophies in the current period. There ought to be a right party if that happens! Get the Queen on to it.

SRC: Perhaps popular fandom will flood back to follow these England teams? People like to support success. We probably always knew that we were not the best, which is also why, historically, some England supporters wanted all the flags and noise and to dominate the action off the pitch and outside the ground. Maybe we were starting to think again in 2019/20 that we are pretty good on the pitch, actually. No need to shout the odds or fight the opposition elsewhere.

JW: But we still have that tension in England between the needs of the Premier League and the national team. We have these young players winning tournaments for England in the underage groups but then getting little or no game time with their clubs. How are they supposed to develop, gain the competitive experience they need, for senior international play?

SRC: There is a lightly strange angle here that one of the very few possible benefits from Brexit is that we might have fewer lower-level foreign players playing in England as a result. Ironically, this could give more chances for our own domestic talent. The difference between having a winning national team and one that is just competing is just a few percentage points. Things might be tilting back just a little bit towards the England team.

JW: Southgate certainly has this calm and measured approach to the manager's job. He doesn't look like he's hating every minute of it, as some England men have in the past. It's actually great that this very likeable, ordinary, intelligent English guy is now leading the way for the game. Intelligence has not always been a master trait for the England boss. To lead a very young team to the semi-finals of the World Cup was an extraordinary performance.

SRC: Being out in Russia, one could see that there may be a power shift coming in the international game. Amidst it all, amidst Brexit and all the world looking on us like we don't know what we are doing with anything except the football, perhaps it is England's time again. *And now there is the Euro 2020 Final, at Wembley, in London.*

CHAPTER 21

The Homes Of Football By Chance

'Gissa Snog' - Everton, 2001
(SRC)

SRC: Just recently, I heard for the very first time, a beautiful song by the American barfly Tom Waits called 'I Hope I Don't Fall in Love with You.' I pounced on it. I took it to be about a guy who has a chance for romance with a good-looking woman in a bar, but her bloke gets in the way. In fact, listening to the song more carefully, he did not stand in their way – I was all too ready to blame someone else for cocking it up oneself. Tom's song was about missing your tilt at the title, in life, because you did not take your chance.

JW: So, taking football pictures at this moment was your fate – this was your main chance, grabbed with both hands. I can see that your pictures can carry so many different messages, just like that brilliant song. You often make us do quite a bit of work as the viewer: 'What's going on here?' The juxtapositions are always really well observed and usually very funny.

SRC: This photograph is of a couple in a clutch having a loving snog outside the Everton ground. The guy is gently cupping his partner's face. One person might look at it and say: 'Oh yeah, it's about a young couple being intimate in public when generally the British are a bit standoffish.' Another may think it's a post-match celebration – a special home win. Or are these lovebirds making up – do they even support the same Merseyside club?

My big sister, in a chiding mood, might believe this shot is more about the onlooking photographer, her brother, who is habitually sidelined, always looking on. Perhaps there is a bit of jealousy here, a man wishing for a special someone to go to the match with.

Some time ago now I also photographed a young woman in Liverpool wearing a full Reds' kit and pushing a pram [page 111]. I intended it as a sideways tribute to a very significant football moment, the dramatic Liverpool Champions League comeback victory over AC Milan in 2005. The Miracle of Istanbul. I took this shot the next day, a wonderfully loyal fan strutting her stuff completely clad in red and who, in my eyes, looked simply great. On social media [Twitter] Full Kit Wankers (that's their handle) seized on the picture as if the purpose of the photograph had been to ridicule this woman when my aim had been the exact opposite. I think most people can see the pleasure and dignity in this photograph, but these guys tweeted it as a prime example of what they are about and their guffawing followers (thousands of them) joined in the joke.

There's nothing much I, who produced the photograph, could do about it. Except shake my head and go red with rage. Throw my toys out the pram.

JW: We see what we want to see, hear what we want to hear, even if sometimes all the king's horsemen and all the social commentators in the world feel like they are dragging us in another direction entirely.

I feel sorry for the Twitter men. Not seeing the incredible pride expressed in that particular picture – my club, my community, my place – is a big loss. It's not difficult to ask someone to look at a photograph, but just don't presume they will see what you see, read it in the way that you read it, spot the subtle subtext. Such is the transaction between the artist and the audience I guess.

SRC: When I came to take each of the photographs in this book, I had all sorts of things swirling around inside of me

causing me to seize on this and that, wait patiently for this and that, exclude from the frame this and that, which then changes the way you are allowed to view it. (Incidentally, I never crop a picture once taken and I never fiddle with its colors. So there's no deception going on.)

I may have viewed these largely unsuspecting folk in my photos as people who I had seen in my youth, members of my family even. Additionally, I may have recalled old monochrome photographs etched in my mind. I wanted to emulate them in my era, on my watch, in my style and in color.

Every single time I press the shutter – on old film cameras where it's a slower, more reflective process – I feel responsible for the picture. It's like I have delivered a new life. I feel a responsibility towards everything I photograph and everything that is football. My chosen subject.

I don't especially want to be in the football dressing rooms – that feels intrusive – yet I do want to be close to my subjects. I want to have the smells and the sounds of the crowd. The people I photograph often want to talk to me, which is lovely, but can also get in the way of taking the photo.

I use standard-vision lenses only so that everything looks exactly how far away it actually was. People have a chance to challenge me, as did that Ipswich skinhead on page 36.

I want to have a kind of conversation with my subjects: *I've got a magic little box; you speak to me and look into it – I need you and you need me to make this picture – and that's the magic.* Everybody is clear what's going on and I feel comfortable with that. Yes, it's surely, almost definitely, a conversation between photographer and subject.

I saw this stylish couple [on page 108] and photographed them and then tweeted about photographing them. They then tweeted back saying they were not in fact a couple but a sister and elder brother, whose family had been coming to Luton Town FC for generations. They said they always, always, always stand in this quirky corner of the ground (beneath a stairwell to the mainstand) before a match.

Here follows a selection of **My Favorite Photos**, preceded by **My Most Popular Photographs** gauged from the public reaction over thirty years. The red pram lady picture is in this *pop* group – and it could have been in the *fave* group as well.

My Most Popular Photographs

'*The Homely Fitba Ground*' - Clydebank, 1989

The boys take charge of the picture, calling the tune.
If taken today, these cheeky chaps might be cheeky girls.
I did not see the gesture until I got the film developed.

'The Kop'
Liverpool, 1992

A formidable opponent if crossed.

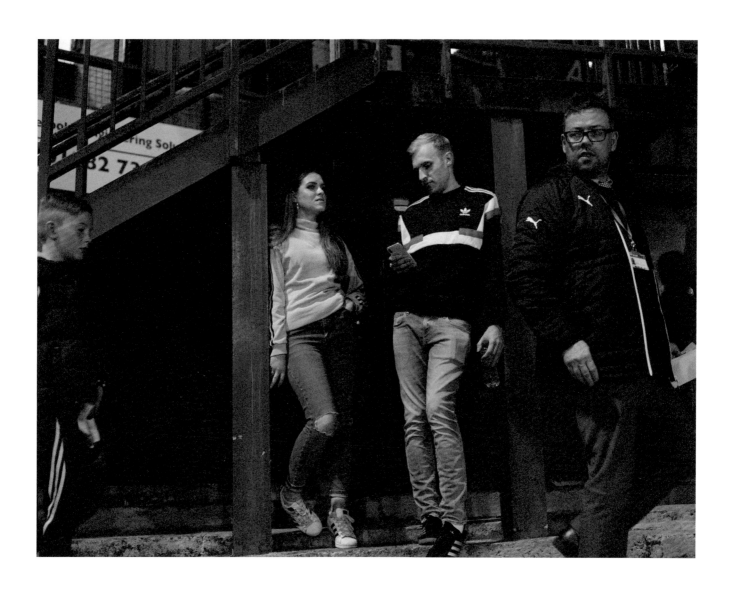

'The Couple That Stand Under The Stairway' - Luton Town, 2019

They are always there.

'Lights Shine On Griffin Park' - Brentford, 2019

It's approaching an end of an era for the west London club. They are moving grounds. In the years to come, all will recall the legend of 'the pub on every corner' in the streets outside the ground.

'*Neon Girls*' - Tranmere Rovers, 1992

Service making you smile.

'*Young Mother Red With Pram*' - **Liverpool, 2005**

The morning after the night before. She might well strut
her stuff, but Father says the baby remains a blue.

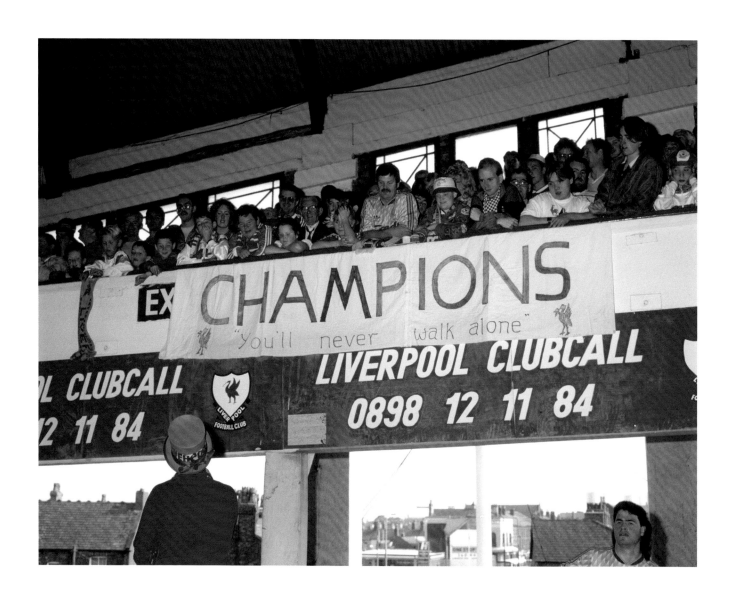

'Up There In The Gods' - Liverpool, 1990

Doctor Fun addresses his champion fans in their loft,
just off to the side from the noisy Kop.

'Meets His Maker'
Waterloo Docks AFC v Collegiate Old Boys, Liverpool 2015

The goalie concedes one.

'Midland's Semifinal Venue'
Aston Villa, 1990

The classic stadium hosts
CRYSTAL PALACE 4, LIVERPOOL 3!
An epoch-changing defeat for the Reds.

'Whereto The Pleasure Of A Man?'
Oxford United, 1990

To the manor born.

'*Back Up The Hill*' - Leeds United, 1990

*The Yorkshire diehards are on a hard walk back
to the top. It's a generation on since they were champions.*

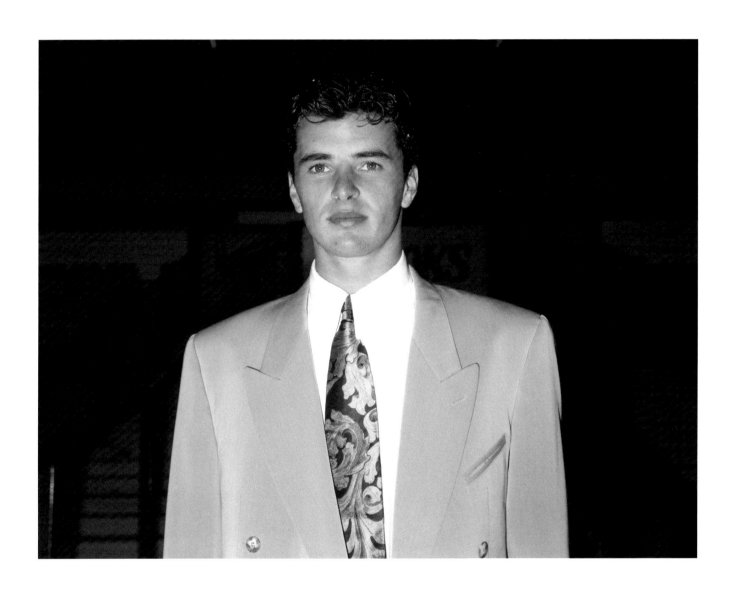

'Gary Speed, Professional Footballer' - Leeds United, 1991

Coming in to his own as a top player.

'*Espying His Likeness*' - Sunderland v Newcastle United, 1992

More than a passing resemblance to...

'*Finding His Likeness In The Crowd*' - **Newcastle United at Sunderland, 1992**

The Goliath player is body-checked.

'A Chicken Is Introduced To The Game' - Blackburn Rovers v Burnley, 2013

Is he about to kick the chicken?

'*Splattered Claret Leaves The Table*' - Burnley, 1991

It's Fourth Division football for him.

'*The Away Lads*'
Newcastle United at Ipswich, 1990

*The heavyweight champions
of Geordieland, on tour in Suffolk.*

'Welcome To Roker Park'
Sunderland, 1990

The steps are worn away in places from years of support.

'Boy On A Roker Swing'
Sunderland, 1991

The lad gets a leg up, above the eyeline of the perimeter advertising hoarding.

'On One Hand' - Sunderland at Portsmouth, 2019

The older you are, the more you may have been through supporting your team.
The last time Sunderland won a trophy of note was 1973, when they beat Leeds United in the FA Cup
final. Even then they were in the Second Division. That was forty-seven years/seasons ago.

'Going Down At Roker'
Sunderland, 1992

*Flying the flag for the final years at a
historic stadium. A Newcastle United fan
is doing a King Kong on the floodlight pylon.*

'*Fog On The Wear*' - Sunderland, 1991

A mist hangs around Wearside.

'Geordies United In The Rain' - Newcastle United v Sunderland, 1992

Major loft conversion taking place at St. James Park.

'We Live On Oakwell' - Barnsley, 1993

*The guard cats Pinky and Perky bunk off their duty
policing Tyke's merchandise.*

'Boy Looks Back Going Home' - **Barnsley, 1997**

*An upward road ahead - hard lessons on a first day's
schooling in the Premiership.*

'Through Thick And Thin' - Swansea City, 1994

Small rear garden with football ground attached.
Docile guard dog provided.

'Shirts On The Line' - **Reading, 1990**

Laundry done next door at a reasonable price.

'Peeling Away Up The Road'
Southampton, 1992

Part-timers beat the referee's final whistle
to get an early start home.

'Looking Up'
Sunderland v Coventry City, 1996

Earning their stripes. Sunderland's brothers and sisters.

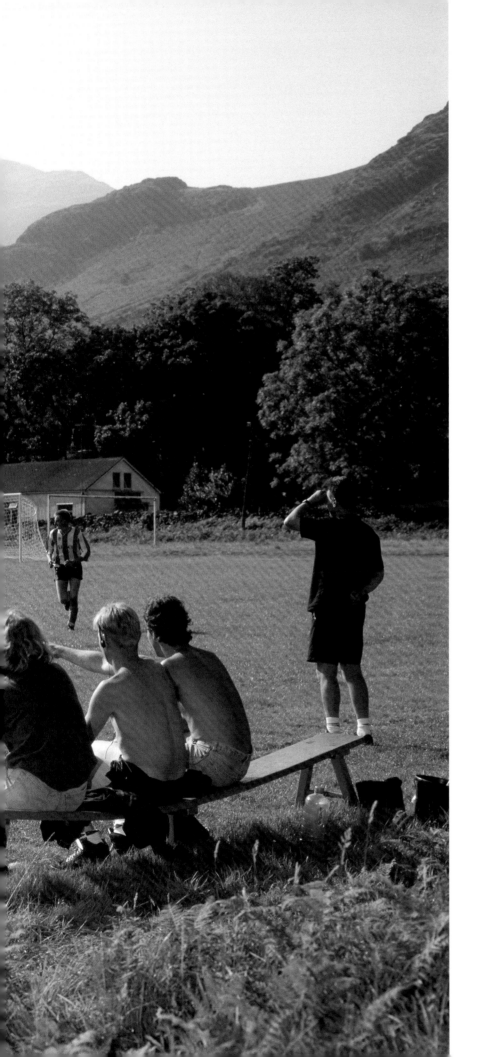

'Home At Shepherdsbridge'
Coniston, 1991

*The locals get their kit off, as
Westmorland League football
returns after the summer break.*

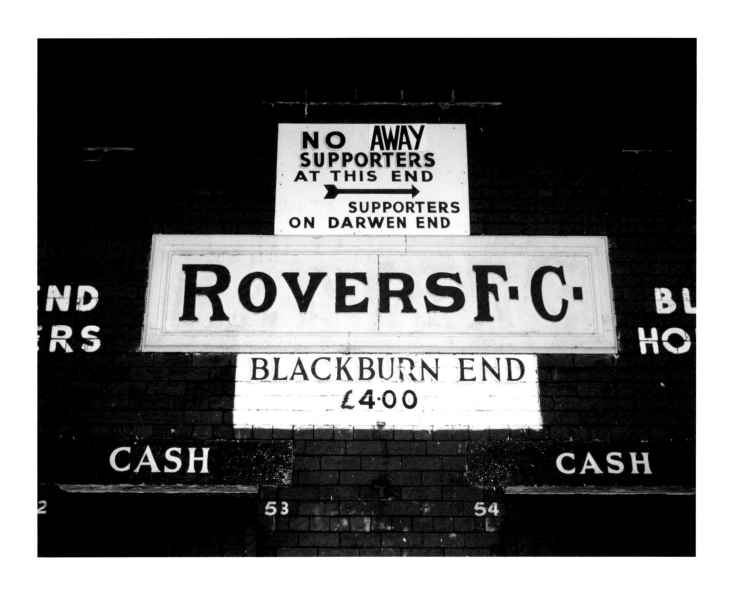

‘*Welcome To Ewood Park*’ - Blackburn Rovers, 1990

*One of the founder members of the League, decked in tiles
and Accrington red brick, sporting reasonable prices.*

'*English Premier League Match*' - Manchester City v Leeds United, 1993

*Names and squad numbers are worn
for the very first time, in the top tier.*

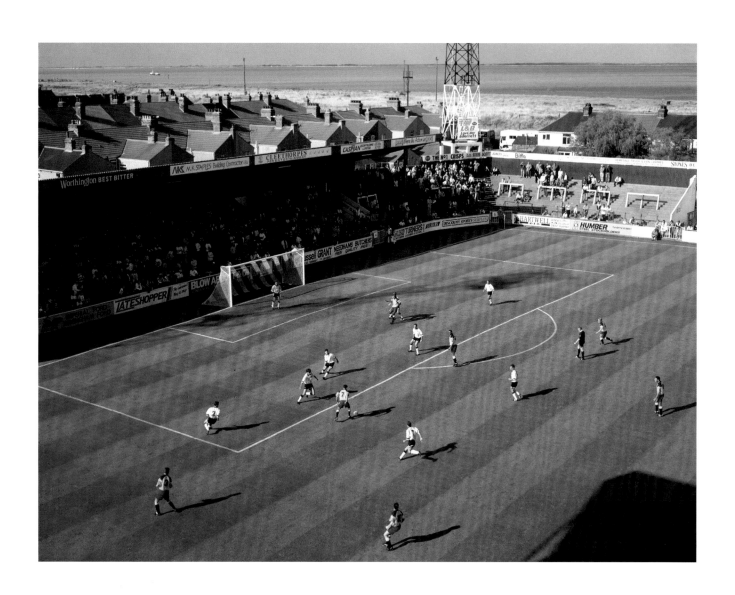

'English First Division Match' - Grimsby Town v Watford, 1993

Nothing happening on the beach. It's all on the pitch.

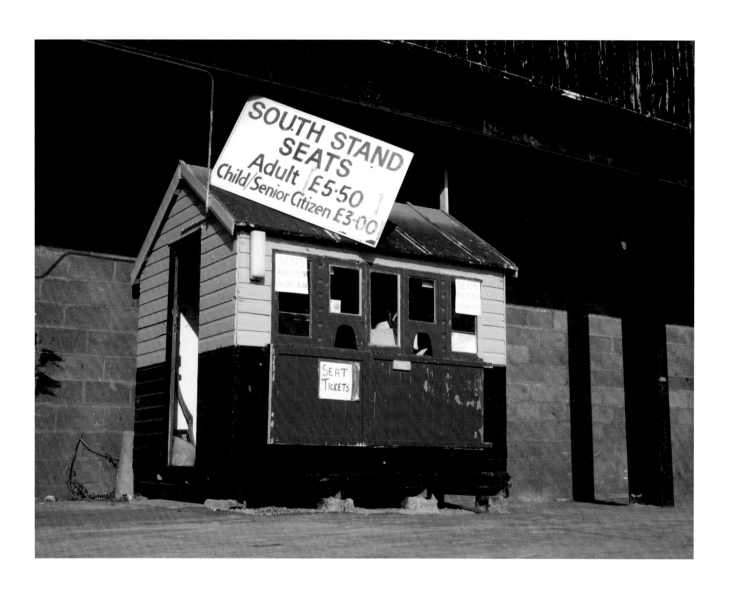

'Ticket Office' - **Hull City, 1990**

*Levitating shed, platformed on stilts,
designed for the flood of ticket purchasers.*

'Experience Surrounded By Youth' - Calver, 2014

The Hope Valley Amateur League team gallantly insists on locals only
- to keep it 'Calver.'

'*Looking To Take The Corner*' - Buxworth, 2014

Having warmed up on the practice pitch, the players get their chance
upon their green carpet of a main stage.

**'A Monumental Storm
Accompanies The Game'
Grimsby Town, 2019**

*The least-followed cup
tournament is poorly attended,
during midweek, against lowly
opposition. The match takes on
biblical proportions as it plays on
through a storm. Dreamlike.
Eventually the referee will pull the
players off.*

'More Than One Match' - Regents Park, 2015

The super sub warms up.

'Higher Noon In North London' - Arsenal v Liverpool, 1990

*Glory of Highbury, Arsenal against
the champions, under a purple sky.*

'Reporting From The Match'
Wycombe Wanderers, 1990

Motson talks a good game - one that
will not be taking place in this weather.

'Standing In The Shadows' - Fulham, 1990

Close encounters of a football kind.

'George Best And Co On The Cregagh Road' - Belfast, 2005

Is this the most talented road in the UK?

'Lights On High Over Elland Road' - Leeds United, 1991

The famous diamond floodlights illuminate the encounter with Everton.

'*Support From Behind The Goal*' - East Stirling, 1996

The hardcore fans. Few were there when Alex Ferguson was manager.

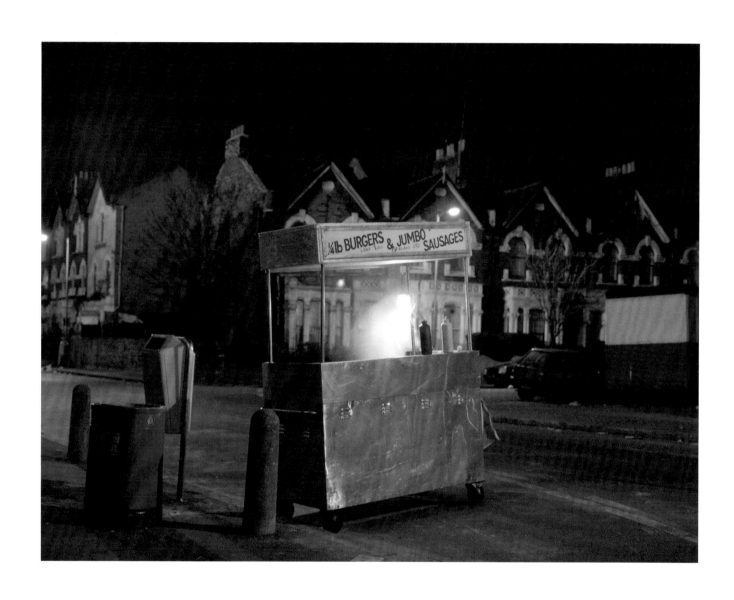

'The Burger Vendor' - Arsenal, 1990

Traditional fayre serving the Hampstead elite.

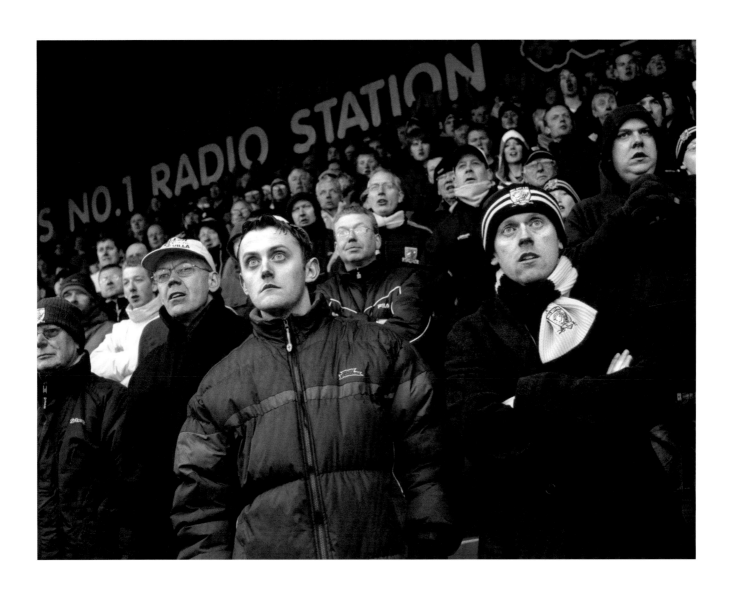

'*Staring Into Space*' - Hull City at Scunthorpe United, 2007

The brothers are surprised.

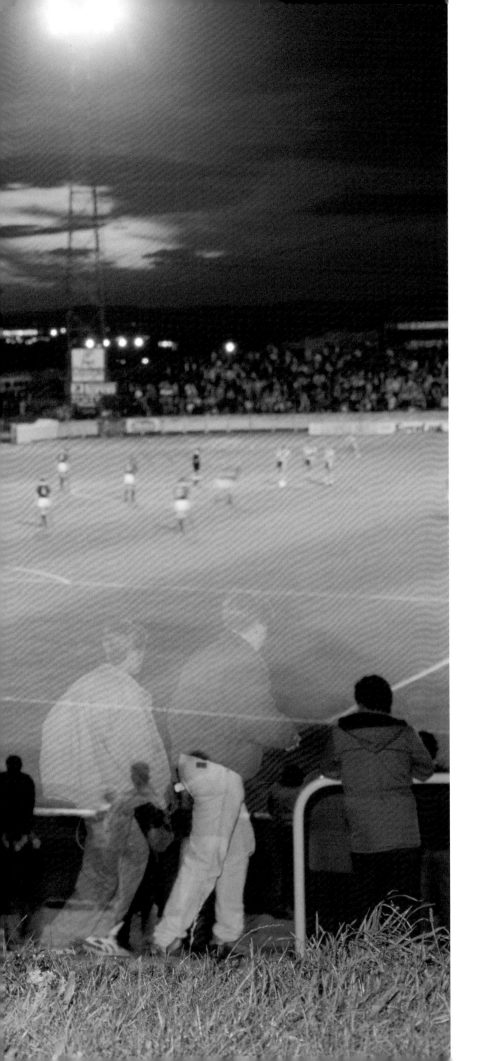

'Sunset Over Springfield Park'
Wigan Athletic, 1990

*The last grassy bank in
English professional football.*

'Leeds Road At Twilight'
Huddersfield Town, 1993

Herbert Chapman's old haunt hosts
Southend United in the cup. I leave the game
and take a walk up the hill. This might not
be here forever.

'Against The Backdrop Of The Big Two'
Hibernian v Heart of Midlothian,
Edinburgh, 1995

Overseen by Arthur's Seat and Salisbury Crags.

'Terracing On Turf Moor' - **Burnley, 1990**

A million and more people have stood here, over time.

'*Climbing That Hill Once More*' - Leeds United, 2019

Every match, win or lose, the trek is made. A pilgrimage.

'*The Mudbank Comes Of Age*' - Manchester United, 1995

*Suspicion is that Liverpudlians are working
overtime at Old Trafford.*

'*Hillsborough Memorial*' - Liverpool, 1990

*A service is held on Stanley Park, between Anfield and Goodison,
on the first anniversary of the disaster that shook the city to its core.*

'Sea Of Green' - Liverpool, 1993

The Spion Kop will soon be seated.

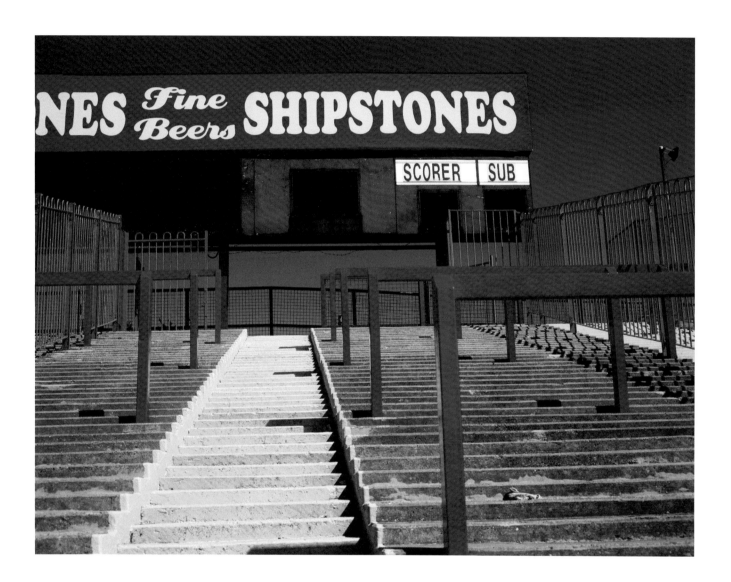

'*Beneath Beer And Blue Skies*' - Nottingham Forest, 1990

The stadium pens will soon be consigned to history.

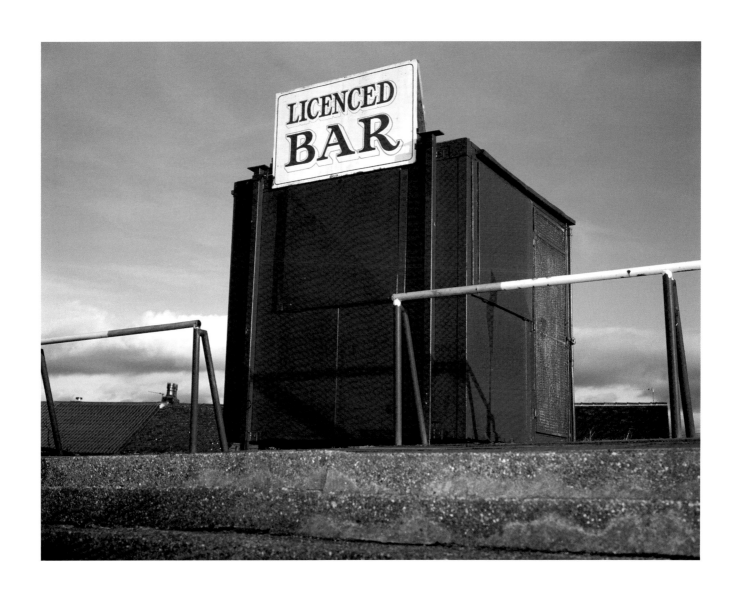

'Refreshment Kiosk' - Leigh RMI, 2005

Inside... the drinking club are having a lock-in.

'*Allegiance To The Wall*' - Rangers at Hampden, 1994

The men like to do what they have always done, together.

'On The Bus' - Rangers, 1996

The fans make their way to Hampden.

'On The Bus With The Cup' - Celtic, 1999

The fans make their way to Hampden.
A blue car comes into view.

'What Do We Think Of...?' - Arsenal, 2014

The club have moved to a striking new stadium,
but the old foe has a familiar name.

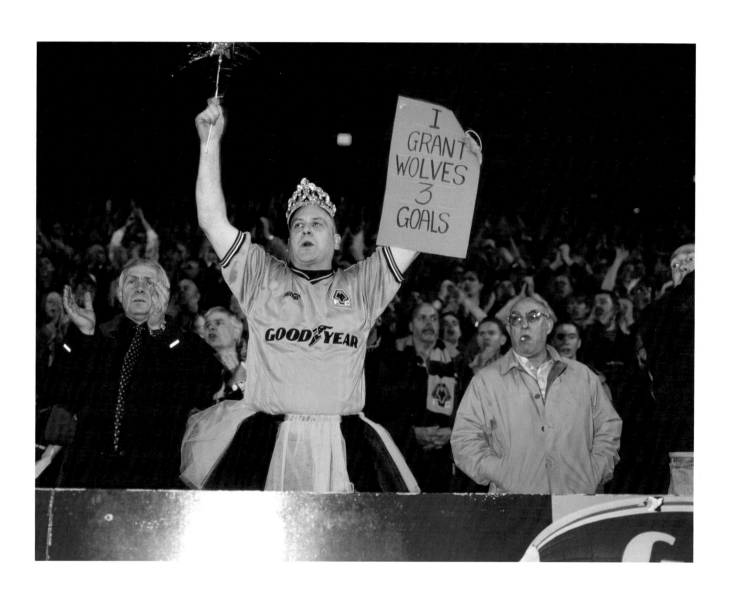

'*Tiara And Tutu Tirade*' - Wolverhampton Wanderers, 2002

They had better win. It's a long haul home dressed like that.

'*The Away Support*' - FC United at Buxton, 2008

Dogged away support for the people's club.

My Favorite Photos

'Boy Peers Round The Wall' - Matlock Town, 2014

*From this position, there is nothing - no fence, no steward,
nobody else much - between him and the football.*

'A Crack At Belle Vue' - Doncaster Rovers, 1990

It was said to be the worst ground in the country. 'A hole.'
But I found a beautiful view. A sliver of England's green.

'Yellow Brick Road' - Bradford City, 1992

The ground has been overhauled, painted up, made magical.
A scene of shocking sadness just seven years before.

'Chairman In Pride Of Place' - **Blackburn Rovers, 1990**

A life given to football, captured inside the trophy room.

'Rose In Her Etihad Tearoom' - Manchester City, 2012

*Photographers, club staff, and a wonderwall of stars - Rose has hosted
everyone in her den under the main stand.*

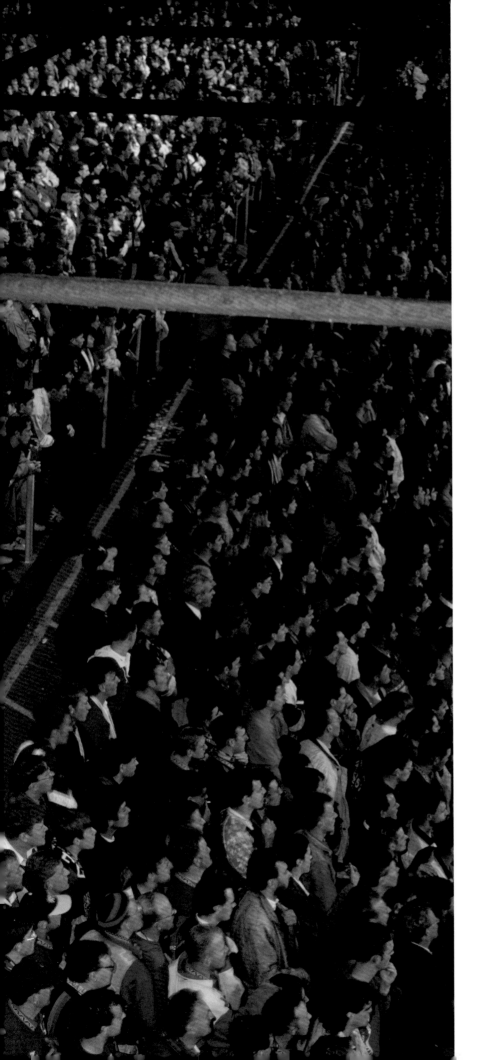

'A Girl Looks Up From The Longside'
Burnley, 1993

The Longside terrace is a coming-of-age
sort of place. A steward checks on his flock.

'On The Move' - **Tranmere Rovers, 1991**

After Leyland Daf defeat a few weeks earlier,
the Rovers find one out of two will do.

'*The Romance Of Early Season*' - Burnley, 1991

Relaxing at a preseason fixture,
before the serious business begins.

'Waiting On The Men Of Ayr' - Ayr United, 1997

Mother and daughter, shopping done, brave the torrent
of turning-out-time at the football.

'*Three Tiers*' - Arbroath at Bo'Ness United, 2014

The generation game.

'Four Lads of South Wales' - Cardiff City, 1994

Did they have a dress rehearsal, or is it synchronicity?

'*Reception Back Home*' - Kilmarnock, 1997

It's cup final day and everyone is going to Hampden.

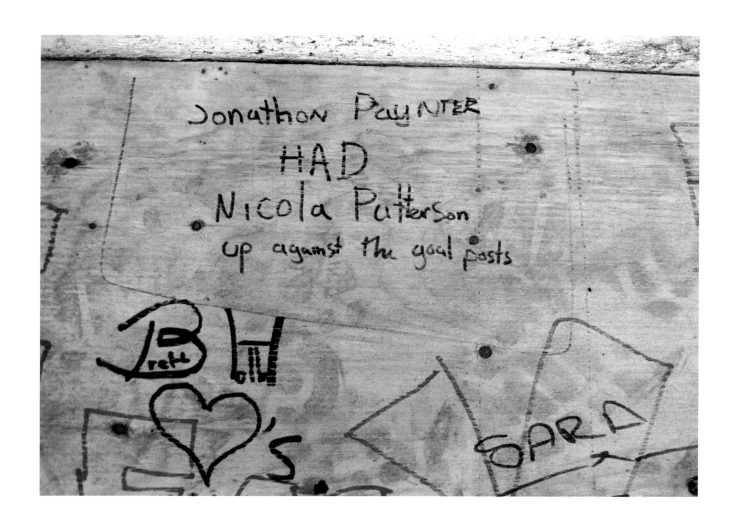

'Graffiti In The Shagging Stand' - Dalbeattie Star, 1996

*After a match, before a match, irrespective of a match being played,
you can break into the Islecroft Stadium and play your own game.*

'*Sombrero Celts*' - Celtic v Rangers, 2008

It's August and everyone is in holiday mood. Irrespective of the score.

'All Along The Mainstand'
Heart of Midlothian, 1993

The Tynecastle ground has a brewery next
door, and when the wind blows its way,
the stand basks in the scent of hops.

'Green Eyes'
Hibernian at Hearts, 2015

The Hibees fill every seat sold
them for the derby.

'Kitty In Her Turban Goes Thru It' - Bradford City, 2015

A tense sporting service, at Valley Parade.

'Lone Huddersfield Town Supporter' - at Southend United, 1993

*His team is struggling in the League with few followers.
And yet, because of segregation, he is made to sit on his own.*

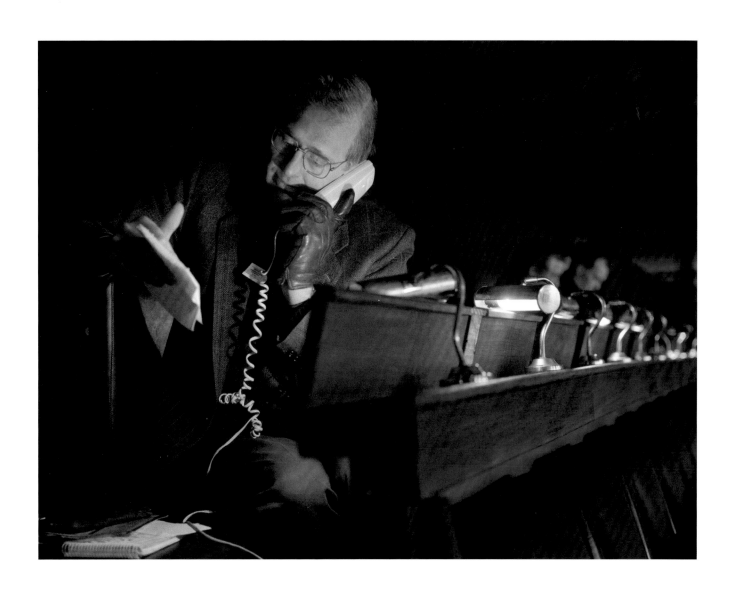

'Filing The Match Report' - **Kilmarnock, 1996**

*The reporter gets to work, telephoning through his words to the newspaper
secretary who will type it up.*

'Romania At A Stroll In The Rose Bowl' - **World Cup USA 1994**

*The USA have done well... but now they are being outplayed on their home
turf, in L.A., before millions of viewers.*

'*Closing The Gap*' - Wolverhampton Wanderers, 1993

*Summer allows a window of about eight weeks to tart the place up,
or even make wholesale changes.*

'Every Word Of The Program Notes' - Buxton, 2014

He has arrived at Silverlands early - as he always does.

'Three Pillars Of Society'
Belper Town v FC United, 2015

*The factory, the church,
and the football.*

'Green And Pleasant Landing'
Ambleside United, 1997

*The football forms an integral
part of the Lake District landscape.*

'Of The Many Great Stadiums' - World Cup Italia, 1990

On the hills outside Rome - another great venue!

'*Mowing Roker*' - Sunderland, 1990

He plays his part, ahead of the team playing theirs.

'*Viewing Elland Road Together*' - Leeds United, 1990

It's a lunchtime appointment to view the
valley's cathedral architecture.

'Best Shirt In The Land'
Dunfermline Athletic, 2013

*It's Christmas-time and there's
still one left in the window.*

'She Wears It Well'
Dunfermline Athletic, 2013

*Best be dressed up for the visit
of Glasgow Rangers.*

'*The Marriage Procession*' - St. Johnstone v FC Lucerne, 2014

*It's early season, July - the team of Perth have a romantic
European date on a balmy Perthshire evening.*

'Face Down Through The Dirty Old Town' - Maidenhead United at Salford City, 2019

Maidenhead have stayed up in the division.
And now they experience Salford up north.

'On The Phone Attraction' - Man City v QPR, 2012

Edgy stuff before the cakewalk crowning.

'The Fat Lady Sings, Dances, Invades The Pitch' - Manchester City, 2012

It's the moment of a lifetime.

'Burst Through The Palace Gates' - Crystal Palace, 1994

Defying everything he has felt before.
Promotion is his.

'Hair Up, Yelling' - Chesterfield, 2014

Promotion is theirs. The League Two title is in reach.

'The Whole Gathering Together' - **Dundee United v Dundee, 2019**

*The two Dundee teams' grounds are 200 meters apart. Truly. The teams walk to the other's
ground when they play each other. On this night it is pouring, lashing down, at Tannadice, yet
altogether providing a match feeling never, ever to be forgotten. And the goals! 6-2!*

'*Sisters Gobsmacked*' - Dundee at Dundee United, 2015

In the process of being hit for six with hardly a reply.

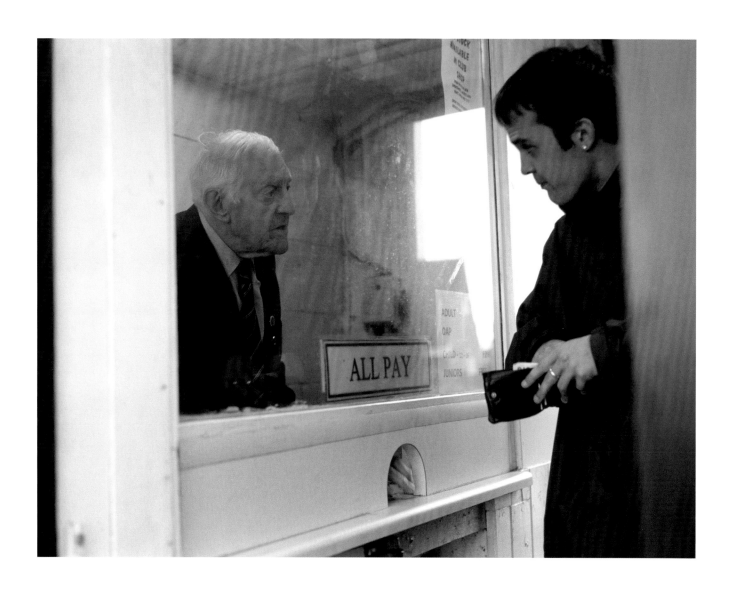

'Everyone Has To Pay' - Stocksbridge Park Steels, 2012

Checking his customer is getting his money's worth.

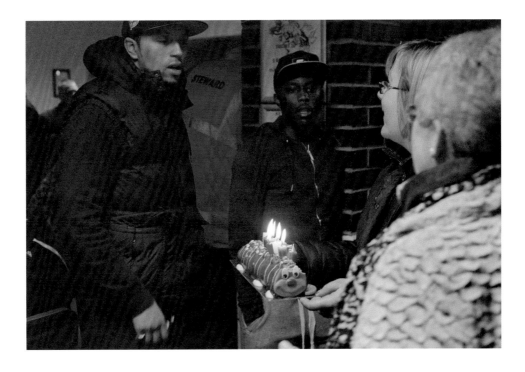

'Losing Out To Wycombe'
Kettering Town, 1991

*Kettering's guests have
overstayed their welcome.*

'Birthday Present Time'
Kettering Town, 2015

*Well meant, but met with
bemusement by the players.*

'Castle And Mound' - Norwich City, 2004

*The fans seek the highest point to celebrate
their city's highest achievement.*

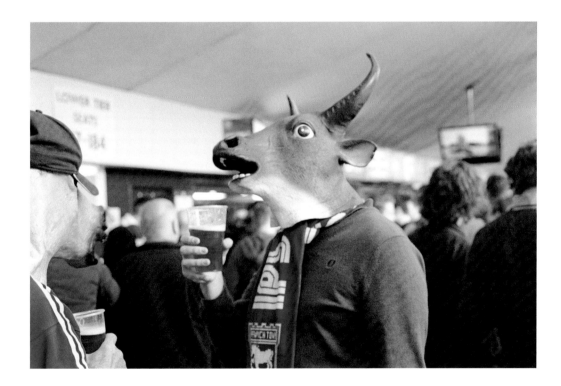

'One Says To The Other'

*'And The Other
Answers The Other'*
Ipswich Town, 2015

*Not every day you get
to play Norwich City.*

'Hanging Out The Washing'
Leeds United, 2012

The men make their way to the game,
going about the houses.

'*Set In Stone*' - Oldham Athletic, 1990

Zoe was in the right place at the right time to etch her name in concrete.

'Breathing Ayresome' - **Middlesbrough, 1991**

A town renowned for its chimneys.

'*Last Day On The Shelf*' - Tottenham Hotspur, 1994

*Everyone has gone home. It's all over for the much loved
stretch of Spurs concrete. It won't be invited back next season.*

'*The Beginnings Of A Forest*' - Nottingham Forest, 1993

The summer allows nature to break back into the City Ground.

'A *New Triumph For T'Town*' - Huddersfield Town, 2017

The younger generation never experienced past successes.
They hold their own against the mighty Manchester City.

'*King For A Day*' - Newcastle United, 1993

*The diminutive Chaplin-esque striker, Andy Cole, is one of the main
reasons the Toon have won their league.*

'Date At The Warwick Road End'
Carlisle United, 2017

The most northerly of Football League
clubs enjoys a day in the sun.

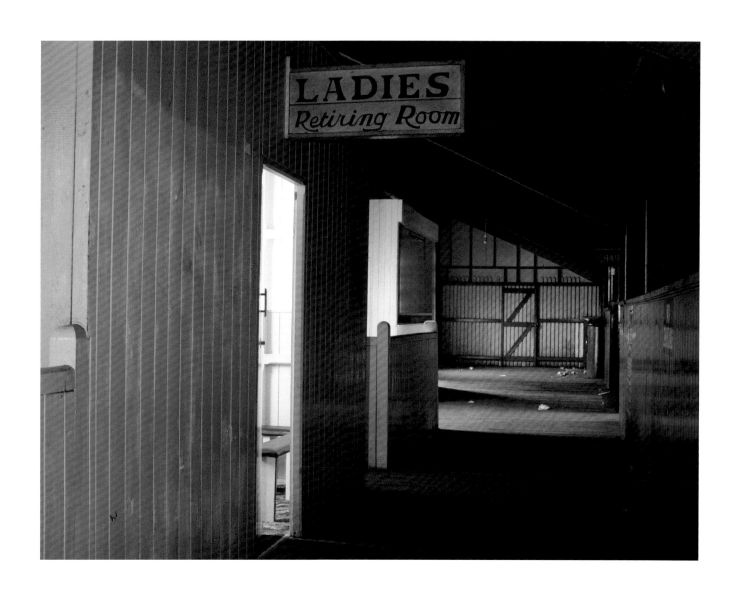

'Ladies Retiring Room' - Bury, 1990

*As the men sit upstairs in the posh wooden seats smoking their cigars and watching
their boys, the ladies are meant to knuckle down to polite conversation and cakes and
ignore thinking about their boys for the span of the match at least. This facility carried
on well out of the Victorian era - and into the 'modern' era.*

'*That Carlisle Jump*' - Carlisle United, 2007

Famous late goals remind one not to leave early from Brunton Park.
A late one against Bournemouth in the fourth Football League tier.

'*Unbelievable Walk*' - Leicester City, 2017

*The humble stroll to the ground will never feel quite the same again
after the 5000-1 league title win of 2015-16.*

'Night Of Great Expectation' - **Sheffield Wednesday, 2017**

The Kop is full to brimming for the Huddersfield playoff encounter.

'The Iron-Man Irony All-Yorkshire Derby'
Sheffield United v Leeds United, 1990

The tough player Vinnie Jones, who has swapped teams and colors and home grounds and fans, gets it in the gob from new teammate and gentle giant Brian Deane.

'Cry For Home' - Greenock Morton, 1995

*His team has beaten the league leaders in the sunshine. But it turns to
rain and cold - and waiting for a bus which never comes.*

'Days Before The Winter Shutdown' - Derby County, 1992

Talk on the street is of a winter break in English football.
What would we do then?

'Woman In Her Youth Walks By'
Buxworth, 2014

A shareholder in the community, no less.

'*Stare-off Before Kickoff*' - Hathersage v Ripley, 2015

The visitors are a man short and are quick to psyche out their hosts.
But it will end in crushing defeat.

'Settled In For The Night' - York City, 2014

They have bags of something for their players.

'*Siege Mentality*' - Grimsby Town at Lincoln City, 2015

The biggest game of their season and paranoia is rife.

'*Sincil Goal*' - Lincoln City v Cheltenham Town, 2015

The Imps are beginning to get their act together
after some barren seasons.

'*The Spring Encounter*' - Mansfield Town at Notts County, 2019

*The Chairman of Notts has unwittingly upped the ante by exposing himself
on social media. The club who were top the season before are now bottom.
Mansfield, the visitors, are top and crowing it.*

'*Shepherds Bush Telegram*' - Queens Park Rangers at Cardiff, 2003

She flashes herself at a moment when her boyfriend's eyes are closed.
He's telling her something profound.
No one else - not even the TV cameras present - have seen this reveal.

'*Header On Goal*' - Notts County v Mansfield Town, 2019

*County, the oldest professional football club in the world,
are under the cosh of their near neighbors.*

'*Pride Of The Rams*' - Derby County v Leeds United, 2019

Derby are in danger of being humiliated by visitors Leeds, hot favorites
to beat Derby to the playoff final.

'City Claim The Occasion' - **Manchester City v Watford, 2019**

*The FA Cup final gives the league winners the chance
to add to their honors for the season.*

'Fan Amidst All That Color' - Manchester City v Watford, 2019

Watford can't be humiliated (in the FA Cup final)
with this manner of support.

'Joy To All The World' - Liverpool, 2019

The team has brought back a European title to Merseyside.

'A German Manager in England' - *Liverpool, 2019*

Klopp in an interview declares thinking about his team 24/7. 'I don't pretend I am interested. I AM interested. It is important to know who you are working with and it's important to know why somebody is determined and motivated.'

'Hands Up Against The Score' - Southampton, 2019

Few win anything in football - no trophies - just a few games here and there.
The game in the UK is a test of our loyalty... Southampton fans absolutely know that they could be
0-5 down at home at halftime, and they would stay on for the second half and be back the very next
match. They are to lose this match 0-9 versus Leicester City. An all-time record defeat.

'Caz And Co Call It' - **Bristol Rovers, 2019**

It's a wonder Rovers have kept going when for so long their fans have been
without their own ground. For seasons on end every match may have seemed
like an away game, which in itself helped forge togetherness.

CHAPTER 22

Behind The Lens

one person.

So the reasons I did all this must be out there – and I propose all of the following reasons put together:

- I was somehow following in my family footsteps.
- I grew up immersed in this world of football.
- Football had an international language and traversed class and snobbery.
- It held a uniquely male index and set of values – something a boy could aspire to.
- I could perhaps right a wrong – football itself seemed to be wronged and heading on a crazy course.
- Someone had to do it – make a portrait of the national game, in such change.
- I just happened to be in the right place at the right time, camera shutter cocked.
- I needed a job – other subjects I was interested in would not find an appreciable audience.

In The Genes And In The Garden

Can I claim this football mission as being an extension of my family trade? My grandfather Clarke, voted in as an 'independent,' held a mayoral role in the 1930s and whilst in office appears to have pursued civic duty rather than 'a political career.' In commissioning sports and recreational facilities he believed he was *doing it for the town*. And what he did is largely still there to see: Butts Meadow football ground is played on most weekends, whilst the open-aired swimming pool (since closed) lives on as a bump in the ground, converted into a skateboard park. As for The Rex – now, officially the finest cinema of any in the country [*The Guardian*] – it looked like curtains when it closed in the 1980s, but it was resurrected.

Growing up in the family house, between the wars, my dad's three elder brothers formed their own football team

Desert island musings: how is it I set out to do just one thing for the peak years of my adult life? For thirty years I have awoken at 5 a.m. and, for a great deal of those 11,000 dawns, have thrown back the covers and gone in search of the football thing when I could have been pursuing life's other pleasures. Photographing for a living, and photographing football especially, sound such fun and hundreds have offered to 'carry my bag' along the way. But alas, I have done most of it on my own and the truth is, it hasn't always been a joyride, and possibly suiting just the

Mother, brother, Stuart at Selsey, Sussex, 1970

and named it after their house: Arosa United FC. My dad looked on, as he was too young to play. Then when they went off to WWII, he made the most of his time, manicuring Arosa's pitch, dragging the roller behind the old car he'd taught himself to drive. He was twelve, thirteen, fourteen, fifteen, and all along running the house alongside an ailing mother. Waiting for the team to start up again, on his brothers' return – when finally he would have his chance to play in their rank.

In turn, when I was growing up, Dad built a full-sized goal in our back garden. All the kids came round to play. He sacrificed the garden and gardening for balls flying all over the place. All summer and winter we would play in 'the Goal.' It could never be neglected, because we owned it: it was part of our family.

Playing The Position Of Observer

My dad then progressed to helping a youth team and then running the entire league. He served every committee role and ended up chairman. I was party to rearranged fixtures, stop-press tales of giant killings, abandonments, punch-ups – generally everything which comes with the territory of parents egging on children in sports. I sat on the stairs overhearing his phone calls – trying to piece together in my mind what could possibly have happened from his side of the conversation, the one I could hear. Sometimes emergency committee meetings were called and held in our dining room. I loved this world. I knew instinctively that this football pursuit, for all its imperfections, was a rightful thing and worth being involved in.

I rarely got a game for the team I was signed up to, in my dad's league. I was invariably substitute. I was at the *wrong* school: one that prioritized rugby and rugby ways over football. My mates still played together at school and quite naturally had a team ready to turn out at weekends as 'Berkhamsted Dynamoes.' I could have felt left out. But rather I grew strong – I became the super-observer. A position I retain to this day.

The Golden Summer Of '77

It was the summer of 1977 when my dad as chairman of the Dacorum Friendly League was asked by Watford FC, through a director who worked for both, if their new manager could be unveiled at his junior football end-of-season awards evening. The manager was not to be BOBBY MOORE but rather a young guy from Lincoln, a northerner, an ex-player retired early from the game through injury. Impressively, Watford Chairman Elton John had personally chosen him.

'Is it alright for him to come along?' came the request. Given that my brother and I would be seated at the head table alongside my dad, we leapt up and said, 'Boy yes! Can he sit next to us?'

We could hardly believe it when the impressive Mr. Taylor (a future England manager) asked us about everything – as if the opinions of a fifteen- and seventeen-year-old really mattered. Graham Taylor doubtless held similar conversations with all and sundry in good time. But my brother and I were the very first to give our diagnosis

The Watford FC team, 1971

SRC's show in Manchester, 2018-19, drew an attendance of 550,000.
(Sean Twamley)

and be impressed by the young Watford manager. In the months that followed I presented him with a picture I had drawn of him. He commissioned more pictures to give to his family. Then Bertie Mee, his more famous assistant, ex of Arsenal, got me to do the same for him. I was bossing it as an artist. *I had a position to play.*

Summer Camp Blues

Having left school and gone to art college, then I went on a summer placement in the USA, to work on a kids' camp. The long days were broken up by occasional games of football, however hot it was. Then when we Brits-abroad-together got the chance to play against another kids' summer camp, we relished the opportunity. But it looked like it would be a one-off, with no more appreciable time off to arrange another game. Our team captain went to see the Camp Lokanda owner… and was sacked on the spot just for asking. We proposed strike action and more: 'If our captain goes we ALL go.' We got our time off. And a few more chances to become a football team.

At summer's end, the camp owner, looking for revenge, challenged us with his USA-select, in front of the entire camp. He himself would go *in gawls*. This meant that he could wear his fancy hat, not get his medallion pulled in a tackle, chat to his adoring crowd. With the match at 1-1, and in its final throes, the ball bounced in front of ME who instinctively booted it high towards that sun and towards the goal vacated by the owner-goalie cockily waltzing about beyond his goal area. Amidst stumblings and a cloud of dirt he emerged helpless, clutching his toupee,

howls of laughter all around. Possibly the greatest team I have ever played in and the most profound sense of victory I would ever experience.

Hitchhiker's Guide

No one could quite believe how I managed to get so many lifts as a hitcher. I even hiked when I didn't need to – when I had my own car in the driveway! I liked thumbing lifts because I wanted to put my trust in other people, and to have them trust me. I am convinced I got so many lifts because I always carried an umbrella. It showed that I cared for myself.

The success of the lifts, which could last hours and hundreds of miles, was in how we spoke to one another. The conversation could always be moved away from awkwardness if we budged it on to the subject of football. Such talk announced and illuminated which town or city one was from. Some people got teary-eyed in these exchanges, recalling floodlights towering over a hometown they left long ago… huddled folk and extended family, all left behind. I even got a lift in an armored car and then an ambulance. And, every time, the talk was about football and roots. This undisputed hitchhiking record of mine: 1,300 lifts in a year was against the background of the Miners' Strike of 1984 and continued right up to the time of 'Heysel' and the 'Bradford disaster' in 1985. All on Prime Minister Margaret Thatcher's watch.

One day, whilst working in a hotel in the remote Lake District (I had hitched to look for work there), I was busy with my chores, including clearing out the fireplaces, when Mr. Lilley, the hotel owner, positioned himself in the big-backed chair in the hotel communal living room. Purposefully drawing on a cigarette, he started flicking through the dozen TV channels, his hand extended, a power play. He paused when it got to some news of a fire at a football match with 'fatalities' – horrific scenes. He carried on puffing, expressionless, flicking through the channels, ignoring my obvious interest in what the BBC was now showing of the Bradford fire. 'Bloody football,' he muttered, waving it away. I was INCENSED.

Working For The Man

Back in my hometown, I was working freelance for local newspapers of the region. Particularly the *Mail*. One week's roster of jobs included my attending the funeral

Stuart's dad's ashes were placed under the cherry tree in the back garden.

of a murdered policeman (who in fact I had briefly known over the years). The family, vetting the list of who would be present at the cemetery, was happy enough for 'the local newspaper' to be represented and pleased to learn that I had personally known their Frank. They were adamant that NO national papers should be present – remarking on how *The Sun* and *Daily Mail* had already been intrusive. I felt a responsibility and I went over in my mind my duties for the day in a way I usually wouldn't have done – after all, this wasn't a local fete or duck race.

I planned the 24 hours ahead: after the funeral I would have the late afternoon and all evening to process the film, make some prints, and deliver them to the paper the next morning. Much like I usually did. No sooner was I home and I got the call from the Hemel office. It was the editor.

EDITOR: Those pictures – could you get them over to us, soonest?
ME: I would prefer in the morning, as planned.
EDITOR: The plan has changed. Lot of interest in them.
ME: I haven't developed them yet and won't do until this evening.
ASSISTANT EDITOR: Can we send a bike over to collect the film then? We will get them printed up.
ME: Eh?… Er, no.
ASST. EDITOR: They are needed NOW for A NATIONAL – they go to print TONIGHT.
ME: But the local paper – ours – was by arrangement with the dead policeman's family to be the only one there.
ASST. EDITOR: That's why they are needed. No one else has them. An exclusive.

ME: No, this is wrong… you can't have them.
ASST. EDITOR: Don't be silly… [at the same time talking to someone else] …we can put a few extra pounds your way – the bike's leaving shortly to come to you.
ME: Well I won't be in! No way. The agreement with the family was just our paper and me!
ASST. EDITOR: [Expletives about me not telling him his business]
--- Call ended. By me. ---
MY DAD: What's going on?
Situation explained.
MY DAD: Stick to your guns.
--- Phone rings. ---
EDITOR: Stuart, this is ridiculous. We have made a deal, we have sold them to *The Sun! THE SUN!* You HAVE to give over the film. BIKE ON ITS WAY! Name your price!
ME: [expletives]
MY DAD: What's going on now?
ME: They're threatening to sack me, if I don't…
MY DAD: Stick to your principles.
--- Phone rings. ---
EDITOR-IN-CHIEF OF WHOLE GROUP: Now, Stuart, I understand there has been a little misunderstanding… but you HAVE to do what we say.

At 9 a.m. the next morning, as I always did, I dutifully dropped off a selection of prints (but not the negatives). EDITOR and ASST. EDITOR are sat there in plumes of cigarette smoke staring me out. It would be months again before I got another job for the paper – the most demeaning they could find from the scrumpled Post-it notes lying beneath their desks. And so it went on, like this, with my being asked to come in and then being humiliated. I had been hung out to dry. I began to imagine working on a larger, long-term photographic commission – where I would be the boss and owner of it, without any compromise.

In Football We Trust: Where I Meet John Williams

John Williams was working for the Sir Norman Chester Centre for Football Research in Leicester when I drove up to see him. On an invite. I had read his stuff and thought he might get mine and lo and behold I was off to meet him. In his small office, he peered over his glasses as if he had, in my photographs, discovered a missing universe. A visual Holy Grail. I am over-egging it, I know, but it is exciting to be 'discovered' and see your instinct you-were-on-to-something validated by a person in office.

John urged that I go on from him and take up with The Football Trust, a body that had money: they were pouring it into concrete projects to rebuild our dilapidated football grounds. And, in his opinion, their rebuilding project lacked a touch of humanity. I had photographs of people using these facilities: grounds built not for one-size-fits-all 'customers' but for humans, with all their faults and idiosyncrasies. John saw a marriage in a kind of heaven for the years to come. The administering authority plus the artist equals prepare the confetti canon. The 1990s were shaping up to be a glorious time.

The Homes Of Football Exhibition And Museum

A simple exhibition grew into a tour (never-ending like Bob Dylan's) and then into a permanent museum for my work: The Homes Of Football At Ambleside In The Lake District. There is a lot of love for what I did there in my thirteen years and even now, years later.

One such – exceptional – validation came a few years in to my mission. I got a call from Wads (the team manager):

'It's Wads; I am on the team bus with the lads.'

'Good for you.'

'And we've had a vote.'

'Good for you.'

'YOU are coming with us to Spain on the team's end of season holiday. Pick you up at 9 a.m. from the end of your driveway.'

Wads' assistant manager Merv had opted out, preferring to spend time with his family. I got his place. Often one hears that a bunch of lads together can be complete, or incomplete, arseholes. This bunch – Carlisle United FC – turned out to be the nicest, warmest, most respectful, playful bunch of lads you could ever hope for. Along the way I have had little problem falling in love with entire clubs, with sets of fans, with individuals in the game – but now I was a little in love with a team. It made me think other squads might be this special if one got to know them. This was another pointer that I should stick with football as my subject.

Moving Home

Recently, when moving house from 61 Egerton Road which included the garden with the goal – indeed the family home of all of sixty-one years and where I was born (no one else had lived there before us), I discovered various things in the loft, as one might expect. Old roller skates my sister wore, etc. But in a bound file marked 'Letters to Football Authorities,' I found various bits of correspondence I never knew my father had. He had written to various shadow/sports ministers and MPs. My dad had railed against the football fan ID membership schemes being proposed, post Hillsborough. And I had never known about these letters. There I was, off on my mission to photograph all The Homes Of Football with quite a bit of fanfare, whilst my dad, a modest man, was on a mission of his own. Again I could see how related we really were, albeit a bit diagonally across a table or an awkward silence for much of the time.

And Daughter

SHE, Ava: the beautiful little daughter of *Mr. Homes of Football*, had got to eleven years of age WITHOUT EVER HAVING BEEN TO A GAME HERSELF! Moreover, she had never even seen a game on TV. A boy (Dylan) had aimed a football at her in the playground and that was the sum of her footy experience.

Then one day it happens. 'Cleethorpes Town FC,' I explain, 'have reached the semifinal!' (I had to explain what constituted a semifinal.) Cleethorpes is her local town. I then thought better of it and suggested we ignore the fixture and go and feed the ducks/go swimming/go to the eat-all-you-can place/go shopping. Shopping would surely do it. Ava eyes me up, purses her lips and utters those magic words: 'LET'S GO TO THE MATCH.' We are in the car. 'Where are all these people going?' she squeals in delight. She eyes their number in disbelief. She says it looks like a pilgrimage. I say Cleethorpes usually get fifty punters but today it could be 2,000 because of the magic of The Cup and the promise of *W-E-M-B-E-R-L-E-Y*. 'They win this and they are at Wembley,' I exclaim. There were other things I had imagined my daughter experiencing with me, Dad, for the very first time in her life: flying, swimming in the ocean, discussing the facts of life… seeing a match.

Nearing kickoff, I revert to type: the football photographer, edging us through the crowd to get us the best viewing position. We crawl through some legs, emerging near the dugout. The 'sponge man,' sensing our purpose, or authority, indicates that we can sit on his stretcher. It becomes a makeshift pitch-side grandstand,

Stuart and daughter Ava, 2020

the best seat in the house – thank you. Driving to the ground I had warned Ava that this would be an arena for swearing – words she might never have heard before or not expressed so forcibly. Now we are here. I point to the manager as a central figure in the opera of swearing that will ensue: 'If the game is going badly he WILL swear. YES, the F-word. Maybe a C-word as well. If, on the other hand, the game is going WELL, he might doubly swear, out of sheer excitement. In fact, if it's boring he might swear even more, just to liven things up.'

There is a goal in the first minute and he's running on the pitch spouting every swear word he has ever known.

One For The Photographers

Should I be training up an heir to continue to do what I have been doing? Will I ever 'retire'? Is it *too late to stop it now?*

Robert Frank, who revolutionized documentary photography in the 1950s, wrote in 2004: 'The kind of photography I did is gone. It's old. There are too many pictures now. A flood of images that passes by, and says, "Why should we remember anything?" There is too much to take in. I am not needed.'

My own tactic where I am needed is to get people to look at more through fewer photos taken – my photos of course – and I try to do this with film, by slowing things down, when the hunger appears to be for digital with its frantic pace.

Desert Island

My desert island was never a desert nor an island but rather in truth a succession of remote or stand-alone houses, where I would retreat and enjoy their privacy and their space. Wherein I could lay out my wares and take another good look at what I had photographed. Piece together the jigsaw. In the background would be music playing, some songs played over and over again, convincing me that I had merely to provide a visual lyricism to life's great soundtrack, almost certainly *already out there.*

'American Girl' - Tom Petty & The Heartbreakers
'Midnight Train To Georgia' - Gladys Knight & The Pips
'Penny Lane' - The Beatles
'Alternative Ulster' - Stiff Little Fingers
'Hitsville U.K.' - The Clash
'Four Strong Winds' - Neil Young
'Romance In Durango' - Bob Dylan
'Cloudbusting' - Kate Bush
'Sweet Thing' - Van Morrison
'Thunder Road' - Bruce Springsteen
'Moon River' - Andy Williams
'Wake Up Everybody' - Harold Melvin & the Blue Notes
'Be You Mighty Sparrow?' - British Sea Power
'Saturday Gigs' - Mott The Hoople

www.HomesOfFootball.co.uk
www.StuartRoyClarke.com

THE GAME

Relegation Books, USA.

An earlier edition of *The Game Revisited*
was published by Bluecoat Press, Liverpool, 2019.

The book came together at:
John's house aside Victoria Park, Leicester
Stuart's chapel house in Louth, Lincolnshire
Mr. G's cafe in Mablethorpe, aside the North Sea.

Designed by Ben Clarke Hickman.

ISBN: 978-0-9847648-9-1
Library of Congress Control Number: 2020932034
Printed in Canada.

Relegation Books LLC
Falls Church, Virginia.
www.relegationbooks.com